**May the Shepherd of your soul bless you.
May He guide, protect, and provide for you as
you lead your family to Him.**

*May "…goodness and mercy follow" you all the days of your life....
(Psalm 23:6)*

THE FAMILY SHEPHERD

Guiding, Serving, and Protecting Your Flock with
Love, Courage, and Enduring Faith

ELI WILLIAMS

THE FAMILY SHEPHERD

Guiding, Serving, and Protecting Your Flock with Love, Courage and Enduring Faith

Published by Movementum Press
www.movementum.com

ISBN: 979-8-9985544-6-9
Revision 2

CONTENTS

PREFACE

The role of a father has never been more critical, nor, perhaps, more confusing. In a culture saturated with distractions and conflicting voices, the spiritual leadership of men in the home is often the last domino to fall. Yet, the biblical mandate for fatherhood — to lead, protect, and instruct — remains timeless.

This book was written in response to a sobering reality confirmed by research. The Manhood Journey's comprehensive *State of Biblical Fatherhood Report*[i], based on assessments from thousands of Christian dads, reveals a profound gap between the faith we profess and the faith we practice in our own homes. The data is clear: a vast majority of fathers have outsourced their primary responsibility.

The report highlights that **78 percent of Christian fathers do not regularly read or discuss Scripture with their children**, and **83 percent do not pray with their families outside of mealtimes or bedtimes**. Even more starkly, **only 26 percent** report spending intentional time helping their children grow in Bible knowledge and spiritual maturity. These are not just numbers about simple disengagement; they point to a discipleship crisis at the very heart of the Christian family. If the next generation is to know and follow Christ, the responsibility lies squarely with the man in the home.

The Family Shepherd: Guiding, Serving, and Protecting Your Flock with Love, Courage, and Enduring Faith is a direct challenge and a practical guide for every man who longs to close this gap. While the statistics may make us feel unqualified or overwhelmed — a sentiment that resonates with the nearly 80 percent of dads who lack consistent spiritual accountability — this book provides the vision, confidence, and tools necessary to embrace the call.

The term "shepherd" is a powerful one. A shepherd doesn't just feed his flock; he protects them from danger, guides them to green pastures, and knows each one by name. This book will illuminate what it means to apply the metaphor of shepherding to leading your family with vision, purpose, courage, and the heart of a servant.

This is not a book demanding perfection; it is a resource that encourages faithfulness in fulfilling a man's highest calling: leading his family in love.

By taking up this mantle — by choosing to shepherd the hearts of those entrusted to your care — you are not just changing your family's trajectory; you are shaping the future of the church, and the community you share. The journey begins now.

DEDICATION

The Family Shepherd: Guiding, Serving, and Protecting Your Flock with Love, Courage, and Enduring Faith is dedicated, first and foremost to Elohim, the Creator of all, and the Designer of the human family. Thank You for portraying Yourself as the Great Shepherd who lovingly watches over, guides and provides for Your people.

To men everywhere who long to lead their families with servant-hearted love, faithful presence, and unrelenting courage as they emulate our Savior, Jesus Christ, the Chief Shepherd. May this book inspire, equip, and encourage you along your fatherhood journey.

ABOUT THE AUTHOR

Eli Williams is the Founder, President, and CEO of Urban Light Ministries, whose programs have included a suite of fatherhood programs that have impacted hundreds of low-income dads in six counties in west central Ohio since the late 1990s. He founded and provides visionary leadership for the annual FatherFest event, his community's annual celebration of fatherhood. The event, now a collaboration with the community's annual Juneteenth festival, includes ULM's Good Dad Awards, which honor men who are doing their best as fathers and father figures. Over the decades, Williams provided the vision for an award-winning community mobilization initiative called Fatherhood Clark County, which promoted healthy fathering county-wide, the Fatherhood Institute, and Urban Light's innovative Fathering Strong[ii] initiative.

Urban Light Ministries (formerly known as Lifeline Ministries) operated The Sonshine Clubs, which were weekly, after-school sessions that provided spiritual enrichment for more than 20,000 public elementary school students in Springfield, Ohio and the surrounding area from 1993 to 2020.

Williams has been married to Judith White-Williams since 1983. Together, they raised her biological son, Elijah, who was three years old when they were wed. Eli adopted Elijah when he was thirteen. Eli has an adult biological son, Joseph, and Judy has another son, Eric.

A now-retired professional broadcaster, Eli's personal ministry began in earnest in April of 1985 when he recommitted his life to Jesus Christ, quit his secular morning radio show on WCOM FM in Urbana, Ohio, and started a Sunday morning Christian music program. Over time, the show morphed into a weekly syndicated gospel music countdown called Hot Gospel 20 that was heard on traditional and Internet radio stations worldwide, until he retired the show in 2021.

Rev. Williams and his wife Judy partnered in a variety of independent outreach and church-based ministries over the years. To better meet the needs of people they ministered to through Urban Light, they planted Fountain of Life Church, and he served as Senior Pastor until the congregation merged with another church five years later. Currently, he is an Associate Pastor at New Hope Church[iii] in Springfield, Ohio, and often fills pulpits of various churches as called upon.

Once an R&B singer and lyricist who wrote a song for Michael Jackson and was the first to record in a studio with EGOT-winner John Legend, Eli Williams has since turned his talents toward a different calling. Today, he bridges the gap between organizational strategy and spiritual ministry, helping pastors and denominations build thriving fatherhood initiatives. Drawing on 40 years of organizational leadership, 35 years as a Christian minister, and 20 years of direct work with fathers, Pastor Williams leverages his 'real-world' perspective to mentor men and advise leadership, ensuring the next generation of 'Family Shepherds' has a clear roadmap to follow.

INTRODUCTION

When my wife and I visited the Holy Land, a simple sight brought a lifetime of Scripture into sharp focus: shepherds, distant figures in the rolling hills, faithfully guiding their flocks.

It was a palpable image that connected me to young David. In my imagination, I could visualize him tending his father's flock and bravely defending the sheep from a lion and, on another occasion, a bear that attacked the flock. He went after the animals, delivered the stolen lambs from their jaws, and when they turned on him, he fought and killed them (1 Samuel 17:34-36).

I thought of the shepherds living out in the fields at night, watching over their flocks. They were the people who were the first to hear the good news of the promised Messiah's arrival as a Holy Babe born in a stable that night in the nearby village of Bethlehem (Luke 2:7-9).

The shepherd is one of the most enduring and beloved metaphors in the Bible — it is the language of God Himself. Scripture is replete with allusions to the Heavenly Father as the Great Shepherd of His ancient people and Jesus Christ as the ultimate Good Shepherd. If spiritual leaders of the Church are called pastors (meaning "shepherds"), how much more must the father, as the spiritual head of his home, embody this role?

Shepherding, at its core, sets forth the biblical model for Christian fatherhood: gentle, faithful, courageous, and sacrificial servant leadership.

This book provides a comprehensive examination of that model. Our journey begins with the vivid reality of a shepherd's life — starting with a fictional Middle Eastern shepherd's story — to explore the critical need for his presence, the heart he must possess, and the specific role and responsibility he embraces. We will closely examine the shepherd's commitment, sacrifice, and servant leadership as we draw inspiration, insight, and practical instruction for godly fathering.

The aim is simple: to equip you, the father, to become the genuine shepherd your family needs, leading them to green pastures and protecting them on life's path.

SECTION I

THE ROLE OF THE SHEPHERD

CHAPTER 1
A Shepherd's Heart: The Tale of Ariel

The biting wind whipped Ariel's worn cloak tighter around him as he stood at the entrance of the stone fold, the last rays of the setting sun painting the Judean hills in hues of purple and gold. His staff, smooth from years of handling, tapped rhythmically against the rocky ground as he counted. "…ninety-seven, ninety-eight, ninety-nine…"

A knot tightened in his stomach. One was missing.

His heart sank. It was young Líra, a spirited lamb with a distinctive black spot over her left eye, known for her adventurous spirit that often led her to nibble grass just a little too far from the flock. "Líra," he whispered her name as a prayer.

Leaving his trusted apprentice, young Barak, to guard the rest of the flock, Ariel grabbed his oil-skin pouch and a torch. The stars were beginning to prick the darkening sky, each one a tiny eye of concern. He retraced the day's path, his sharp eyes scanning the broken ground for any sign — a bent blade of grass, a dislodged stone. He called out, his voice hoarse against the rising wind, "Líra! Líra!"

Hours passed. The moon, a sliver of silver, offered little light. Ariel's mind raced, picturing the dangers: a rocky crevice, a thorny bush, or worse, the glint of a predator's eyes. He scaled a small ridge, the familiar bleating of sheep a distant memory. Then, he heard it—a faint, trembling "Baa!" from below.

He scrambled down into a shallow ravine, his torch casting dancing shadows. There Líra was, wedged between two rocks, her small legs caught, whimpering. She had pushed through a thicket, likely seeking a particularly tasty clump of herbs, and fallen. The brush had scraped her side, and a thorn had pierced her ear, making her tremble.

Ariel's heart swelled with relief. He carefully freed her, checking for serious injury. She was shaken and a little bloody, but her bones seemed sound. He pulled out a small pot of healing oil from his pouch and gently rubbed it into her scrapes, whispering soft, comforting words. Then, he lifted her, light as a feather, placing her over his shoulders, her small legs crossed over his chest, feeling the warmth of her trembling body against him.

The journey back was slow, Ariel carefully navigating the treacherous terrain, Líra's breath a soft puff against his neck. By the time he reached the fold, the first hints of dawn were painting the horizon. Barak met him, his face etched with worry, which melted into a relieved smile at the sight of Líra. Ariel placed the lamb gently inside the fold, where she quickly found her mother.

He collapsed by the entrance, exhausted, but with a profound sense of peace. Every sheep mattered.

Battling for His Flock

Days turned into weeks, and Líra healed, her adventurous spirit undimmed, though she stuck closer to the flock now. One twilight evening, as Ariel led his sheep toward a familiar watering hole, an unnatural stillness fell over the air. The sheep, usually bleating about, grew quiet and still, their heads lifting, ears twitching.

Ariel knew that feeling. It was the scent of danger, carried on the breeze. He scanned the rocky outcrops, his hand instinctively gripping his staff. Then he saw it—a gaunt, grey wolf, its eyes burning with predatory hunger, crouched low on a nearby rise, its gaze fixed on the fattest lamb at the edge of the flock.

There was no time for thought, only instinct. With a battle cry that startled the sheep into huddling closer, Ariel launched himself forward, placing his body between the wolf and his flock. The wolf, surprised by the shepherd's sudden charge, hesitated for a split second.

That was all Ariel needed. He swung his heavy staff with all his might, aiming for the wolf's head. The wolf, quick as lightning, dodged, snapping its jaws within inches of his arm. Ariel felt the rush of air, the hot breath of the beast.

The fight was a blur of growls, grunts, and the thud of the staff. Ariel knew he wasn't fighting for sport, but for the lives entrusted to him. He remembered his father's words: "The shepherd stands between the wolf and the lamb." He thrust the staff forward, keeping the wolf at bay, circling, trying to force it away from the scattered, frightened sheep.

The wolf, emboldened by hunger, feinted left, then lunged right, attempting to slip past Ariel to the vulnerable flock. Ariel pivoted, swinging the staff like a long baseball bat, catching the wolf hard on its flank. A yelp of pain erupted from the beast, and it stumbled back, its predatory glint replaced with a flicker of injured surprise.

Seeing its advantage lost, and perhaps sensing the shepherd's unwavering determination, the wolf turned and disappeared into the deepening shadows, a grey specter swallowed by the encroaching night.

Ariel stood panting, his muscles aching, his heart pounding a frantic rhythm against his ribs. He gripped his staff, its tip still pointing towards the direction the wolf had fled. He was unharmed, except for a few scrapes and the exhaustion of battle, but more importantly, his flock was safe.

He slowly walked back to the terrified sheep, who were now huddled together, their eyes wide. He knelt amongst them, stroking their wool, murmuring reassurances. He was their protector, their guide, their very gate in the night. The fight had been personal, a testament to the sacred trust placed in his hands, and a vivid reminder of the shepherd's endless watch.

Questions for Reflection and Discussion

A Shepherd's Heart: The Tale of Ariel

- **The Missing Lamb:** Ariel immediately noticed the absence of **one** lamb, Líra. As a father, how well do you know the distinct nature and current state of **each** of your children? Can you name one recent incident where you noticed a subtle, but significant, shift in one child's behavior or mood?

- **The Relentless Pursuit:** Ariel left the ninety-nine in the care of his helper, Barak to pursue the one lost lamb, sacrificing his rest and risking his safety in the dark.

    o   Do you have a coparent? If so, in what specific ways are you and your child's mother working hard at being a good **shepherding team**?

    o   In what ways do you currently **sacrifice** your personal comfort, time, or resources to pursue a child who seems to be drifting, struggling, or moving away from the "flock"?

- **Wounds and Comfort:** When Ariel found Líra, she was scraped, pierced by a thorn, and trembling. He didn't just bring her back; he applied **healing oil** and offered **soft, comforting words**.

    o   What are the "thorns" (wounds, hurts, or bad influences) that your children might currently be struggling with?

- How do you ensure you are applying "healing oil" (comfort, gentle correction, unconditional love) before you attempt to carry them back to safety?

- **The Weight on the Shoulders:** Ariel carried Líra "light as a feather" on his shoulders. What are the specific **burdens** (academic pressure, social issues, emotional struggles) that your children are carrying right now, and how are you physically or emotionally bearing that weight *with* them, rather than expecting them to manage it alone?

Battling for His Flock

- **Sensing the Danger:** Ariel sensed the "unnatural stillness" and "scent of danger" before he even saw the wolf. What are the subtle signals or **"scents"** that tell you danger (negative influences, harmful habits, questionable friends) is near your family? How can you sharpen your awareness of these threats?

- **Standing in the Gap:** Ariel's instinct was to immediately launch himself forward, placing **his body** between the wolf and the flock. What are the major "wolves" (cultural pressures, technological dangers, toxic attitudes) currently preying on your children?

  - What concrete, physical actions (e.g., controlling access, changing environments, intervening in conversations) are you taking to stand directly in the gap as a protector?

- **The Battle Cry:** Ariel let out a "battle cry" that startled the wolf and mobilized the sheep to huddle. What does your "**battle cry**" look and sound like? Is it a loud, clear declaration of your family's values, or is it a quiet, inconsistent whisper?

- **Unwavering Determination:** The wolf fled because of Ariel's "unwavering determination." Reflect on a recent conflict or challenge related to protecting your children. Was your determination **unwavering**, or did you retreat too quickly in the face of resistance or difficulty?

- **After the Fight:** After the wolf fled, Ariel "knelt amongst them, stroking their wool, murmuring reassurances." How quickly do you transition from the **protector/disciplinarian** role to the **comforter/nurturer** role once a threat is past or a disciplinary action is complete? Why is this transition essential for a child's sense of security?

CHAPTER 2
Why Shepherds are Necessary

Sheep possess virtually no natural defenses or survival instincts, meaning their very existence hinges on the competence, diligence, and presence of their caregiver.

The profoundly dependent and vulnerable nature of sheep fundamentally illustrates the vital importance of a good shepherd by creating a relationship of absolute necessity.

Here is how their nature underscores the shepherd's importance:

The Sheep's Vulnerabilities

Sheep are uniquely ill-equipped to survive on their own, highlighting the indispensable role of the shepherd in four key areas:

Helplessness Against Predators

Sheep are defenseless. They lack powerful claws, sharp teeth, or the speed to outrun major predators, such as wolves, bears, or lions. When threatened, their instinct is often to scatter or freeze, making them easy targets.

The Shepherd's Role: The shepherd is the sole protector and warrior. He must be courageous, equipped with a rod and staff (weapons), and willing to risk his life to fend off attacks, embodying the Good Shepherd, Jesus the Messiah, who lays down his life for His sheep (John 10:11).

Inability to Find Sustenance

Sheep lack the instinct and intelligence to consistently find and choose safe food and water. They will graze until they are malnourished on poor grass or drink from running water, which terrifies them, often leading to illness or death.

The Shepherd's Role: The shepherd serves as both the provider and guide. He must know the terrain to lead them to "green pastures" and "still waters" (Psalm 23:2). This highlights the shepherd's wisdom and knowledge as essential for the flock's health and sustenance.

Lack of Self-Correction (Prone to Straying)

Sheep are notorious for wandering off the path, not out of malice or rebellion, but simply due to distraction. Once lost, a sheep often panics and cannot find its way back. Furthermore, if they fall on their backs (a condition known as "being cast"), they cannot right themselves and will die if not rescued.

The Shepherd's Role: The shepherd is the attentive restorer. He must be vigilant in his counting and searching, using the staff to hook and guide straying animals gently. Such care demonstrates the necessity of personal, proactive intervention to save the helpless, emphasizing that guidance is an act of rescue.

Overwhelming Fear and Panic

Sheep are naturally fearful and require a constant sense of security to thrive. They won't even lie down to rest unless they feel completely safe.

The Shepherd's Role: The shepherd is the source of security and comfort. His voice calms them, and his physical presence eliminates their anxiety. The promise, "I will fear no evil, for you are with me" (Psalm 23:4), encapsulates the idea that the shepherd's presence alone is the key to the sheep's peace.

To illustrate sheep's utter dependence upon, and trust in, their shepherd, read this former fighter pilot's eyewitness account.

As a young man, I served my country in the Air Force. I was a Weapon Systems Officer in the F-4E Phantom II jet fighter-bomber. I flew 180+ combat missions in Southeast Asia. If asked if God had saved and protected me, I would have said "Yes, certainly. We once brought back an airplane with part of a wing missing, and the time we scraped the treetops." God had His purpose in these events, but He had another object lesson for me.

Later, I was flying in Turkey. We would take off from Incirlik Air Base (at the northeast corner of the Mediterranean), fly over the Tarsus mountains, and go to a practice bomb range at Konya (where Paul was beaten and kicked out). On the return flight, we passed over a large, central arid area. The region was sparse – a few huts, a few crops, and lots of sheep.

From 20,000 feet, we could see flocks of sheep grazing and decided to have some fun. We dropped down to our minimum allowed altitude to buzz the sheep. Now the F-4 is a LOUD airplane, trailing clouds of ominous black smoke. Not understanding, the sheep perceived they were under attack by giant, ugly birds of prey – they sought safety and protection. This is what I witnessed: the sheep ran to their shepherd, converging into a massive ball of wool at his camp. They believed and trusted in him.

Now I get it. The sheep <u>knew</u> their shepherd and absolutely trusted him for their safety and protection. The shepherd <u>knew</u> his sheep and would give his life to protect them. How thrilling to know, as a sheep, I have a Shepherd who knows me and gave His life for me. Through faith, belief, and trust in my Good Shepherd, Jesus, I am truly saved and under His protection.

In summary, the sheep's total vulnerability means the shepherd is not merely a caretaker but the source of their life, safety, and direction. The fragility of the flock makes the shepherd's diligence and character the most critical factor in their survival.

Questions for Reflection and Discussion

The Sheep's Vulnerabilities: Recognizing Dependence

- **Helplessness Against Predators (The Warrior):** The sheep's only defense is the shepherd. As a father, what areas of your children's lives are you **delegating** protection to others (school, media, friends) that you should be personally and actively **guarding**? What "rod and staff" (tools, rules, and courage) do you need to employ to stand between them and a current "predator"?

    - *For Discussion:* Discuss the difference between **shielding** your children from all pain versus **protecting** them from moral/spiritual harm.

- **Inability to Find Sustenance (The Guide):** Sheep will starve themselves on poor grass and drink from terrifying running water. Where are you currently leading your family for **sustenance** (intellectual, spiritual, relational food)? Are you guiding them to **"green pastures"** (healthy habits, faith, stable relationships) or simply letting them graze haphazardly on whatever is easiest or most convenient?

    - *For Reflection:* Identify one "still water" (a place of calm, rest, or spiritual focus) you can establish for your family this week.

- **Lack of Self-Correction (The Attentive Restorer):** Sheep are easily distracted and, if "cast" (fallen on their backs), cannot save themselves.

- o Which of your children is currently most **"distracted"** and wandering off the established family path? How are you using your **staff** (gentle, proactive guidance) to hook and guide them back before they panic and get truly lost?

- o What are the signs that a family member is **"cast"** (overwhelmed by despair, burden, or sin) and needs immediate, hands-on rescue and restoration, not just advice?

- **Overwhelming Fear and Panic (The Source of Security):** Sheep won't rest unless they feel secure. What are the major anxieties or fears your children express? Does your **presence** and **voice** automatically bring them peace, or does it sometimes add to their anxiety?

The F-4 Phantom II Object Lesson: Absolute Trust

- **The Reaction to the Threat:** When the LOUD F-4 jet fighter buzzed the flock, the sheep didn't scatter; they **ran toward the shepherd** and converged into a massive ball of wool at his feet.

  - o When an unexpected crisis or loud danger (financial pressure, major conflict, uncertainty) hits your family, what is your children's **instinctive reaction**? Do they turn **toward you** for safety and explanation, or do they retreat and scatter?

- **Earning Trust:** The sheep's reaction proves their **absolute trust** in their shepherd's protection. As a father, how do you intentionally build the kind of trust that makes your children's immediate reaction in a crisis to run *to* you?

- o *For Discussion:* What is one thing you did this past week that built trust, and one thing you did that may have eroded it?

- **The Shepherd's Character:** The chapter concludes that the shepherd's **diligence and character** are the most critical factor in the flock's survival. Beyond providing financially, what is one area of your **character** that you are actively working on (patience, consistency, integrity) because you know your family's safety and well-being depend on it?

CHAPTER 3
A Day in the Life of a Middle Eastern Shepherd

The life of the biblical shepherd was not one of leisure, far from it. His days and nights required constant vigilance, long hours, and personal risk. **It was an endless watch and a big responsibility.**

The Value of Sheep

Sheep were a true capital asset. Attempting to estimate the worth of sheep in today's dollars is complex because determining the value of an item from the time of David (around 1000 BCE) involves multiple, widely varying methods and interpretations. The value depends not just on the price of silver, but also on the **purchasing power**, that is, what a sheep represented to an ancient family or economy.

One perspective is to consider the sheep's value in relation to a day's or month's wage, as livestock represented significant capital and sustenance. In one context (though later than David), a sacrificial animal could cost the equivalent of a **month's wages for an average laborer.**

If we assume a minimum modern monthly wage of roughly **$2,000 - $4,000**, the value of a single, unblemished sheep could be in that range.

However, it's crucial to understand that for David's family, the **economic significance** of a sheep, which provided wool, milk, meat, and was an essential unit of wealth and sacrifice, was far greater than its simple cash price to a modern person.

Clearly, shepherding was **essential work.** His job was to protect the sheep at all costs, even his life. **The ancient shepherd was often a low-level warrior!**

The Shepherd's Weapons

While the **rod** (a short, heavy club, often with a mace-like head) and the **staff** (a long stick, sometimes with a crook for guidance and rescue) were the primary tools, here are the other key weapons ancient shepherds carried:

1. The Sling (The Projectile Weapon)

The most famous weapon, beyond the rod and staff, is the **sling** (Hebrew: *qela*), famously used by David to defeat Goliath.

- **Description:** It was a simple, yet incredibly effective weapon made of a small leather or woven pouch attached to two long cords (often made of wool or sinew).

- **Ammunition:** The shepherd would carry a **bag** or pouch filled with smooth, stream-bed stones — the ideal, readily available, and aerodynamic ammunition.

- **Purpose:**

    - **Defense:** Used as a lethal projectile weapon against predators (like lions, bears, and wolves) or human rustlers/raiders. A skilled slinger could launch a stone at speeds over 60 mph, powerful enough to break bone.

- **Guidance:** Used to guide the flock by slinging a stone *near* a straying sheep to startle it back into the flock, without necessarily hitting it.

2. The Dagger or Knife

While not always explicitly mentioned in pastoral scenes, a sharp blade was an essential multi-purpose tool and weapon for survival.

- **Purpose:**
    - **Processing:** For cutting up meat, skinning animals, and trimming wool.
    - **Defense:** Used for close-quarters combat against large predators or thieves if the sling or club failed, or as a last-resort sidearm.

3. The Ox Goad (Used as an Improvised Weapon)

While primarily an agricultural tool used for driving oxen, the goad could be a formidable weapon.

- **Description:** A long wooden pole, often about eight feet long, with a sharp **iron spike or point** on one end (to prod animals) and a flat metal scraper on the other (to clear dirt from the plowshare).

- **Biblical Example:** The Judge **Shamgar** is recorded as defeating six hundred Philistines with nothing but an **ox**

goad (*Judges 3:31*), showing its potential as a devastating weapon.

In summary, the ancient shepherd was equipped not just for tending, but also for defending the flock as if it were a military unit, relying on the **rod** for heavy, close-range defense, the **sling** for accurate long-range attacks, and a **dagger/knife** for close-quarters utility and survival.

He was a fierce protector, yet a gentle leader of the sheep. The shepherd was not a driver who walked behind the flock, for sheep were not pushed like cattle. The shepherd was a leader who walked **before** them, always in sight. Sheep are too short to see the pasture ahead, so they rely on the shepherd to guide them. That's literal **servant leadership**.

Sunrise: The Call to Lead

The shepherd's day begins before the sun rises, following the rhythm of nature, not a clock.

- **The Shepherd's Voice:** The shepherd leads the sheep out of the safety of the fold (a stone enclosure or cave). He calls out with a unique, familiar sound, and **his sheep follow him** (John 10:3–4). They know his voice and trust his direction.

- **The Path Chosen:** The shepherd's first task is to select the day's route, carefully choosing paths that offer both safety and sustenance. That requires deep knowledge of the land, weather, and potential dangers. He walks ahead, determining every step the flock will take.

Midday: Provision and Nurture

The daylight hours of the shepherd are spent actively fulfilling the duties of provision and care.

- **Seeking Green Pastures:** The shepherd guides the flock to grazing lands, ensuring the grass is of good quality to keep the sheep healthy. He makes them lie down in the pastures, often because they will not rest unless they are entirely secure.

- **Leading to Still Waters:** Sheep are terrified of fast-moving, running water. The shepherd must lead them to quiet, slow-moving pools or draw water for them from a well so they can drink and be refreshed. This requires patience and gentleness.

- **Attending to the Vulnerable:** The shepherd constantly checks the flock for injuries or diseases. He pays special attention to the lambs and nursing mothers, often **carrying the weakest lambs close to his chest or in his arms** to protect them from the arduous journey (Isaiah 40:11).

Evening: Accountability

As the heat subsides and evening approaches, the risk increases, demanding focused attention for the journey home.

- **The Journey Back:** The shepherd guides the tired flock back to the temporary or permanent sheepfold. This path is often dangerous as predators begin to stir.

- **Counting Under the Rod:** At the entrance of the fold, the shepherd stands, and as each sheep passes through the narrow opening, he **counts them one by one, often using his rod to touch and inspect each animal gently (Leviticus 27:32).** This is the moment of **accountability** — ensuring that none are missing or injured.

- **Treating Wounds:** Any sheep that is wounded, sick, or exhausted is tended to immediately upon entering the safety of the fold.

Night: Sacrificial Watch

The night brings the most significant risk and demands the shepherd's ultimate commitment.

- **The Gatekeeper:** In a simple sheepfold (often a stone circle or cave), there is no literal wooden gate. The shepherd usually **lies down across the narrow entrance**, becoming the living gate himself (a literal act of self-sacrifice, echoing John 10:7, 9).

- **Protection at Personal Risk:** Throughout the dark hours, the shepherd stays awake, on guard against predators (such as wolves, bears, and lions) and human thieves. It is a lonely, cold, and dangerous shift that requires **courage, vigilance, and a readiness to fight** — just as young David fought a lion and a bear for his flock (1 Samuel 17:34-37).

- **Long-Term Dedication:** The shepherd's job is often a migratory one, leading him away from home for weeks or months. It is an occupation of **solitude and ceaseless**

dedication to the welfare of the flock, as their dependency is absolute.

The Father's Parallel

The life of the shepherd is a profound picture of selfless, 24/7 care. The father, like a shepherd, is constantly on call, not driving his family, but lovingly **leading** them, knowing that their survival and flourishing depend on his intimate knowledge, courage, and faithful vigilance. We will flesh that out later. Keep reading.

In the next chapter, let's examine the ultimate example of shepherding set by Father God Himself.

Questions for Reflection and Discussion

The Value and Tools of the Shepherd

- **Capital Asset:** The sheep represented a family's significant **wealth and sustenance** — a capital asset worth far more than its cash price. As a father, do you treat your children (and their well-being) as your most valuable, non-negotiable asset? How would your daily priorities change if you mentally assigned them the *value* of a life-long investment that must be guarded at all costs?

- **The Leader Who Walks Before:** The shepherd is a **leader** who walks **before** the flock, not a driver who pushes from behind. In what areas are you actively **leading by example** (walking the path first) versus merely **driving** (giving orders and expecting compliance)?

- **The Rod (Close-Range Defense):** The rod is a heavy club for fierce, close-quarters combat and defense. What are the **core family values and non-negotiables** that you protect with the Rod — that is, the clear, unbending discipline or final "No" you are willing to use to defend your family's safety and moral integrity?

- **The Sling (Long-Range Guidance):** David used the sling for long-range defense but also for **guidance** (to startle a sheep back into the flock). What is your **long-range guidance system** (teaching, stories, media choices, traditions) that you use to gently correct your children before they are in immediate danger, without having to "hit" them with harsh, last-minute intervention?

The Shepherd's Endless Watch: A 24/7 Commitment

Sunrise: The Call to Lead

- **The Shepherd's Voice:** The sheep know and follow the shepherd's **unique, familiar voice**. What does your distinct "father's voice" communicate to your children? Is it a voice of consistent peace, firm direction, hurried stress, or frequent anger?

- **Choosing the Path:** The shepherd proactively chooses the day's path for **safety and sustenance**. Are you intentionally choosing your family's **"path"** (daily schedule, weekly activities, media consumption) or are you simply reacting to external demands and letting the current of the culture carry you along?

Midday: Provision and Nurture

- **Leading to Still Waters:** Sheep are terrified of running water, requiring the shepherd to lead them to **quiet, still waters**. What "running waters" (fast pace, over-scheduling, constant noise, uncertainty) currently cause fear and anxiety in your children? What tangible steps can you take this week to establish a few moments of **"still water"** (calm, focused presence) for your family to be refreshed?

- **Attending to the Vulnerable:** The shepherd constantly checks the flock, often carrying the **weakest lambs** close to his chest. Who in your family (a child, a spouse) currently feels like the "weakest lamb" — the one most fragile, overwhelmed, or overlooked? What specific action will you take this week to carry their burden and protect them from the arduous journey?

Evening and Night: Accountability and Sacrifice

- **Counting Under the Rod:** At the fold, the shepherd counts and gently inspects each sheep **under the rod** — a moment of personal accountability. What is your daily **"under the rod"** moment with your children? Is it a specific time (bedtime story, dinner talk) where you ensure every family member is checked, counted, and accounted for before the day ends?

- **The Gatekeeper:** In the night, the shepherd lies down across the entrance, becoming the **living gate** (John 10:7, 9). What personal **sacrifice** are you currently making (of sleep, leisure, entertainment, or privacy) to literally or figuratively guard the entrance of your home against the dangers of the night (whether they are physical or digital)?

  - *For Discussion:* David fought a lion and a bear alone at night. What is one area where you need to cultivate **lonely courage** — fighting a threat to your family even if no one else is watching or applauding?

CHAPTER 4
The Heavenly Father as the Divine Shepherd

We have been referring to the 23rd Psalm. Now, let us consider how, in it, verse by verse, King David, the former shepherd boy, lyrically describes God's loving care for Him as his Divine Shepherd.

The Lord is my shepherd;

I shall not want.

2 He makes me to lie down in green pastures;

He leads me beside the still waters.

3 He restores my soul;

He leads me in the paths of righteousness

For His name's sake.

4 Yea, though I walk through the valley of the shadow of death,

I will fear no evil;

For You are with me;

Your rod and Your staff, they comfort me.

5 You prepare a table before me in the presence of my enemies;

You anoint my head with oil;

My cup runs over.

6 Surely goodness and mercy shall follow me

All the days of my life;

And I will dwell in the house of the Lord

Forever. - Psalm 23

I grouped Psalm 23 into four stanzas—the first three focus on aspects of the Great Shepherd's care. The final one is David's faith-filled response. Let's go!

Stanza 1 – Provision

The Lord is my shepherd;

I shall not want.

2 He makes me to lie down in green pastures;

He leads me beside the still waters.

3 He restores my soul;

He leads me in the paths of righteousness

For His name's sake. – Psalm 23

David wrote and sang this praise of the LORD God for being his Shepherd who faithfully provided for all his needs. In the first stanza (verses 1-3), David expressed absolute confidence that just as a human shepherd makes sure the sheep have plenty of tender grass to eat, quiet water from which to drink, and a safe place to sleep comfortably, Jehovah Jireh ("The Lord my provider") would be the supplier of all his daily needs.

He had no lack of food, water, or rest for his body or soul as he followed His Shepherd's leading.

Stanza 2 – Protection

4Yea, though I walk through the valley of the shadow of death,

I will fear no evil;

For You are with me;

Your rod and Your staff, they comfort me. – Psalm 23

David felt complete safety and security as he followed his Divine Shepherd through dark and dangerous passages where evil lurked, not even fearing death (verse 4). His assurance came from knowing his Shepherd was near and armed with a powerful rod and staff.

The rod is a short, heavy club, often with a knob on the end, sometimes studded with nails. The staff was long enough to keep predators at a distance. With those weapons, a shepherd fights off wild animals and human predators that threaten the sheep. David was comforted knowing his Shepherd would never use His weaponry against him, but to bludgeon his enemies.

Stanza 3 – Blessings, and Healing

5 You prepare a table before me in the presence of my enemies;

You anoint my head with oil;

My cup runs over. – Psalm 23

Blessings

In verse 5a, David wrote and sang about having a Shepherd who provided him with a banquet of spiritual blessings, even though his enemies surrounded him. While his foes, both the four-legged and two-legged kind, were seeking to destroy him, Jehovah Jireh was providing everything David needed in abundance as they watched. "In yo' face!" kids might say.

Healing

During the course of the day, sheep can get cuts on their heads from certain plants due to their sharp burr-like structures. They are also in danger from pests that can infect their eyes, nose, and ears.

As a shepherd pours oil upon the head of the sheep to heal their physical injuries and to protect them from parasites, David, despite being a king, continually experienced wounds and dangers, making spiritual "oil" a personal necessity for him. In verse 5b, David testified to the Great Shepherd's tender loving care.

- **Soothed Wounds:** David suffered intense emotional and psychological wounds from numerous crises: Saul's relentless pursuit, the loss of his son, and the weight of his own sin (e.g., the affair with Bathsheba). God, as his Shepherd, provided the "oil" of forgiveness and emotional restoration to soothe his guilt and heal his spirit. The oil represents God's tenderness in binding up the wounds of His deeply flawed but repentant servant.

- **Protection from Pests:** David was constantly harassed by "pests" - his enemies (both foreign and domestic, like Absalom). The oil covering his head represented God's protective presence, shielding his mind and spirit from the debilitating fear and distraction caused by those who sought his downfall. It assured him that God was actively defending his thoughts and peace.

The Ministry of the Holy Spirit

Oil is a biblical reference to the Holy Spirit. The ceremonial act of anointing with oil symbolized setting apart a person or object for a particular purpose. David was anointed king by Samuel when he was a boy.

I believe David sang praises to God out of gratitude that the spiritual oil of God was overflowing upon him. He rejoiced in the abundant reassurance that the Holy Spirit's presence, power, and favor were upon his life and kingship, honoring him, despite his enemies' desire to destroy him.

Stanza 4 – Faith-Filled Finale

6 Surely goodness and mercy shall follow me

All the days of my life;

And I will dwell in the house of the Lord

Forever. - Psalm 23

The constant tender loving care, provision, guidance, and protection of the Great Shepherd so overwhelmed David that he, in complete confidence, declared that his eternal future was secure (verse 6).

David concluded the song with the faith-filled proclamation that his Shepherd's unmerited favor would never leave him. He was without doubt that as long as he faithfully followed His Shepherd, he would be continually surrounded by His abundant goodness and loving kindness for the remainder of his days on earth.

Then, after being pursued by God's goodness and unfailing compassion throughout his earthly life, the Great Shepherd would welcome him into His heavenly home to live with Him forever.

Summary

The Psalmist depicted Almighty God, in whose image we are created, as the Divine Shepherd. It is an appropriate and beautiful way of illustrating the gentle, caring, and nurturing nature of our God. A metaphor that was easily understood by the people of the time.

Other Examples

Other Old Testament scriptures portray the Heavenly Father as the Great Shepherd.

- **Genesis 48:15 NIV:** (Jacob's blessing) …" *May the God before whom my fathers Abraham and Isaac walked faithfully, the God who has been my shepherd all my life to this day...*"

- **Psalm 80:1 NIV:** "*Hear us, Shepherd of Israel, you who lead Joseph like a flock. You who sit enthroned between the cherubim, shine forth.*"

- **Isaiah 40:11 ESV:** "*He will tend his flock like a shepherd; he will gather the lambs in his arms; he will carry them in his bosom, and gently lead those that are with young.*"

- **Ezekiel 34:11-12 NKJV:** "*For thus says the Lord God: 'Indeed I Myself will search for My sheep and seek them out. As a shepherd seeks out his flock on the day that he is among his scattered sheep, so will I seek out My sheep and deliver* *them from all the places where they were scattered on a cloudy and dark day.'"*

- **Jeremiah 31:10 NKJV:** *"Hear the word of the Lord, O nations, and declare it in the isles afar off, and say, 'He who scattered Israel will gather him, and keep him as a shepherd does his flock.'"*

Questions for Reflection and Discussion

Stanza 1: Provision and Guidance (The Lord is My Provider)

- **No Want (Verse 1):** David declares, "I shall not want." As a modern father, what are you teaching your children to truly "want" (or prioritize)? Is your focus on providing them with **material abundance** or on guiding them toward the **spiritual provision** and contentment found in following God?

- **Green Pastures and Still Waters (Verse 2):** God's guidance ensures rest and refreshment. How often do you consciously step back from your own busy life to ensure your children have literal and figurative **"green pastures"** (time for rest, creative play, healthy relationships) and **"still waters"** (moments of calm, reflection, or focused spiritual input)?

- **Restoration and Righteous Paths (Verse 3):** The Shepherd **restores the soul** and leads in **paths of righteousness**. When your child is spiritually or emotionally drained, what practices or conversations do you use to facilitate the "restoration of their soul," rather than just trying to change their bad behavior?

Stanza 2: Protection and Presence (The Valley of Fear)

- **Fear No Evil (Verse 4a):** David's security came from the Shepherd's **presence** ("You are with me"). How do you actively communicate your comforting, protective presence to your children, especially when they are walking through their personal **"valley of the shadow of**

death" (e.g., anxiety, academic failure, social exclusion, serious illness)?

- **The Rod and Staff as Comfort (Verse 4b):** David found **comfort** in the Shepherd's weapons. Do your children view your authority (your "rod" of discipline and your "staff" of direction) as instruments of **comfort and security**? Or do they see them primarily as instruments of fear or unpredictable anger?

    - *For Discussion:* Discuss a time when your firm boundary or correction (your "rod") actually brought a child relief because it defined their safe limits.

Stanza 3: Blessings and Healing (Anointing with Oil)

- **Table in the Presence of Enemies (Verse 5a):** The Shepherd provides a banquet even while enemies watch. What are the **spiritual blessings** or signs of God's grace in your family's life that are undeniable, even to those who may be hostile to your values? How do you make sure your children **notice and celebrate** this "prepared table" of blessings?

- **Anointing with Oil (Verse 5b):** The oil represents healing for physical/emotional wounds and protection from "pests" (harassment/anxiety).

    - What are the modern "thorns and pests" (guilt, media pressure, comparison) that require you to apply the **"oil of forgiveness and restoration"** to your children?

o   As a father, how do you seek out and receive the
spiritual "oil" (forgiveness, comfort, Holy Spirit
guidance) for your *own* emotional wounds and
exhaustion so that you can pour out care, not
depletion, onto your family?

Stanza 4: Faith-Filled Finale (A Secure Future)

- **Goodness and Mercy Shall Follow (Verse 6a):** David
  was confident that God's favor would **follow** him. How
  does the unwavering promise of God's **goodness and
  mercy** affect how you respond to your children's failures,
  mistakes, and rebellions? Are you quick to extend mercy,
  reflecting the Divine Shepherd's nature?

- **Dwell Forever (Verse 6b):** The final confidence is eternal
  security. What is one specific, intentional practice you
  incorporate into your family life (reading, prayer, service)
  that points your children, and reminds yourself, of the
  ultimate hope of **dwelling in the house of the Lord
  forever?**

  o   *For Reflection:* This chapter provides a clear
  model for fatherhood. Identify one verse from
  Psalm 23 that you will try to **live out** more
  faithfully in your home this week.

CHAPTER 5
The Significance of God as Shepherd

The shepherd metaphor is the most comprehensive symbol for the Triune God's relationship with humanity because it merges **absolute power with ultimate tenderness**.

The depiction of God the Father and Jesus the Son as a Divine Shepherd is important. **What does that have to do with pastors and you as a father?** Let's investigate the first part of that question next.

The Heavenly Father as the Great Shepherd

Know that the Lord, He is God;

It is He who has made us, and not we ourselves;

We are His people and the sheep of His pasture. – Psalm 100:3

The Father, as the Shepherd of ancient Israel, sets the foundational covenant of Providence and Ownership.

- **Absolute Ownership:** The Father's shepherding establishes that the people (Israel/believers) **belong entirely to Him** (Psalm 100:3). He is the Creator and Sustainer, meaning His care is not contractual but intrinsic to His nature.

    - **Significance for Pastors:** This means pastors, as under-shepherds, **do not own the flock**. They are merely stewards. Their loyalty must be to the

Owner, following His directions for the care of the sheep.

- **Complete Provision:** The Father ensures total provision, safety, and direction (Psalm 23). He is the source of "green pastures" and "still waters."

    - **Significance for Pastors:** Pastors are called upon to rely on God's provision and His Word to feed the flock, not on their own inadequate strength or resources.

Jesus Christ, The Son as the Good Shepherd

The theme of Jesus Christ, the Son of God, as a Shepherd is also prominent in the Holy Scriptures.

This is what Jesus declared about Himself:

"I am the good shepherd. The good shepherd gives His life for the sheep." – John 10:11

The Son's role establishes the standard of **Sacrificial Leadership and Intimate Relationship**.

- **Sacrificial Commitment:** Jesus Christ is the Good Shepherd who *"lays down his life for the sheep"* (John 10:11). This is the radical, ultimate measure of care, distinguishing Him from the hired hand who flees when danger comes.

    - **Significance for Pastors:** This sets the standard that pastoral leadership is fundamentally about

selfless sacrifice and courage in the face of
spiritual danger, not self-preservation or comfort.

- **Intimate Knowledge and Voice:** Jesus emphasizes, "I
  know my sheep and my sheep know me" (John 10:14).
  His relationship is personal; the sheep follow because
  they recognize His unique, trustworthy voice.

  - **Significance for Pastors:** Pastors are called to
    cultivate an intimate, personal relationship with
    the members of their flock, knowing them and
    their struggles by name. More importantly, they
    must ensure their own teaching (their voice) is
    clearly recognizable as the voice of Christ,
    directing the sheep only to Him.

- **The Shepherd as the Gate:** Jesus declares, *"I am the gate
  for the sheep"* (John 10:7). He is the sole entry point to
  salvation and the sole source of security and protection.

  - **Significance for Pastors:** Pastors must always
    point their flock to Jesus Christ as the only means
    of salvation and the sole true source of eternal
    security. They guard the entrance, ensuring that
    the flock is protected from false teachings.

More References to Jesus as the Good Shepherd

Here are several other key scriptures that reference this:

- **John 10:16 NKJV:** *"And other sheep I have which are not of
  this fold; them also I must bring, and they will hear My voice;
  and there will be one flock and one shepherd."*

- **Hebrews 13:20 NKJV:** "*Now may the God of peace who brought up our Lord Jesus from the dead, that great Shepherd of the sheep, through the blood of the everlasting covenant...*"

- **1 Peter 2:25 NKJV:** "*For you were like sheep going astray, but have now returned to the Shepherd and Overseer of your souls.*"

- **1 Peter 5:4 NASB:** "*and when the Chief Shepherd appears, you will receive the unfading crown of glory.*"

- **Revelation 7:17 NKJV:** "*For the Lamb who is in the midst of the throne will shepherd them and lead them to living fountains of waters. And God will wipe away every tear from their eyes.*" (The Lamb, referring to Jesus, acts as the Shepherd)

The Holy Spirit: The Indwelling Divine Guide

Following the profound care of the Heavenly Father and the sacrificial love of Jesus, the Good Shepherd, the Holy Spirit completes the Triune care for the believer. The Holy Spirit is the **Indwelling Divine Guide**, ensuring that every child of God (a sheep of the Divine Shepherd's fold) receives perfect, constant, and internal attention. His ministry fulfills the highest functions of a caretaker — leader, teacher, protector, and source of empowerment.

The Spirit as Leader: Directing in Righteousness

The Holy Spirit acts as the believer's inner **Leader**, continually directing the heart toward God's ultimate purpose and safety. This assures that the Lord "leads me in the paths of righteousness" (Psalm 23:3). The Spirit's leadership is both moral and directional, enabling the believer to follow a course that honors God.

- **Scripture Reference (Galatians 5:16):** "I say then: **Walk in the Spirit, and you shall not fulfill the lust of the flesh.**" The Spirit is the divine power that enables believers to resist temptation and follow a righteous path, ensuring moral and spiritual well-being.

- **The Internal Guide:** The Spirit acts as an internal, dynamic **Guide**, prompting immediate course correction when the believer stumbles or makes a wrong turn. He guides with perfect precision, prompting conviction when we wander and gently redirecting us toward God's will (Romans 8:14).

The Spirit as Teacher: Illuminating Christ's Truth

A good leader instructs his followers, and the Holy Spirit serves as the believer's definitive **Teacher** and source of spiritual illumination. His divine function is to ensure that the depth of Christ's teachings is not merely heard, but understood, remembered, and applied.

- **Scripture Reference (John 14:26):** "But the Helper, the Holy Spirit, whom the Father will send in My name, **He will teach you all things, and bring to your remembrance all things that I said to you.**" The Spirit guarantees that all truth revealed by Jesus is accessible and actionable for the believer.

The Spirit as Protector and Comforter: Constant Presence

The Spirit is the constant presence of God in the believer's life, fulfilling the dual needs of spiritual protection and emotional comfort.

- **Scripture Reference (Psalm 23:4):** "Yea, though I walk through the valley of the shadow of death, **I will fear no evil; For You are with me; Your rod and Your staff, they comfort me**." As the Comforter (John 14:16), the Spirit offers profound peace in the midst of life's deepest trials, acting as God's personal assurance and spiritual defense.

The Spirit as Anointing: Empowerment and Authority

The Old Testament tradition of anointing with oil symbolized healing, protection, and commissioning. The Spirit's **anointing** is the spiritual reality of this practice, signifying the indwelling God's healing touch, divine authorization, and endowment of power.

- **Scripture Reference (Acts 1:8):** "But you shall receive power when the Holy Spirit has come upon you; and you shall be My witnesses in Jerusalem, and in all Judea and Samaria, and to the end of the earth." This empowerment is the divine commissioning that equips the child of God not only to be blessed ("my cup runneth over" (Psalm 23:5) but to effectively represent and serve the Great Shepherd, enabling them to perform the "greater works" (John 14:12) of ministry.

Questions for Reflection and Discussion

The Heavenly Father: Absolute Ownership and Provision

- **Ownership vs. Stewardship:** The Father's shepherding establishes that He has **Absolute Ownership** over the flock. As a father, do you view your children as your **possessions** (to be controlled and molded for your benefit) or as a **sacred trust** (sheep you are stewarding for God, the true Owner)?

    - *For Reflection:* How does knowing you are a **steward** change how you discipline, guide, and plan for your children's future?

- **Relying on God's Resources:** The Father, as the source of **Complete Provision**, calls under-shepherds (pastors and fathers) to rely on His resources and His Word. When facing a deep need or crisis in your family, are you seeking "green pastures" from the **world's resources** (money, power, status) or relying on the **provision and wisdom found in God's Word**?

Jesus Christ: Sacrificial Leadership and Intimate Relationship

- **The Standard of Sacrifice (John 10:11):** Jesus sets the standard that the Good Shepherd **"gives His life for the sheep."** What are the most difficult or painful **sacrifices** you have recently made for the safety, well-being, or spiritual health of your family that reflect Christ's selfless love, rather than simply fulfilling a duty?

- **The Shepherd as the Gate (John 10:7):** Jesus is the **sole Gate** for salvation and security. How intentionally are you pointing your children toward **Christ alone** as the source of their worth, their safety, and their eternal hope?

    - *For Discussion:* What does it look like for a father to **guard the gate** against "false teachings" and worldly philosophies that seek to influence his children?

- **The Intimate Voice (John 10:14):** Jesus knows His sheep and they know His voice. How well do you **intimately know** the individual hearts, fears, and internal struggles of each of your children? More importantly, is your teaching **(your voice)** consistent with the teachings of Christ, so that when your children hear you, they recognize the direction of the Chief Shepherd?

The Holy Spirit: The Indwelling Divine Guide

- **Internal Course Correction (The Spirit as Leader):** The Holy Spirit is the internal Guide who prompts **immediate course correction** when a believer stumbles. As a father, how often do you pause to ask the Holy Spirit to guide your decisions, your words, and your actions **before** you address a child's behavior, ensuring you are leading them in the "paths of righteousness" (Galatians 5:16)?

- **Empowerment for Service (The Spirit as Anointing):** The Spirit's anointing is for empowerment and authority (Acts 1:8). Do you pray for the Holy Spirit's **power and authority** to rest upon your own life and upon your children's lives?

- *For Reflection:* David's "cup runs over" (Psalm 23:5) with God's blessing. How are you encouraging your children to use their overflowing spiritual blessings and gifts **to serve** others, instead of keeping them for themselves?

- **Teaching and Remembrance (John 14:26):** The Holy Spirit teaches and brings **remembrance of Christ's truth**. What practices (family devotion, Scripture reading) are you implementing to fill your children's minds with God's Word, so that the Holy Spirit has the truth necessary to teach and comfort them in moments of trial?

CHAPTER 6
Pastors as Under-Shepherds

The Father, Son, and Holy Spirit establish the perfect model of shepherding: leadership rooted in ownership, sustained by total provision, proven by selfless sacrifice, and constant presence.

The Divine Shepherd metaphor is the theological lens through which we understand the pastoral calling.

When we turn now to the New Testament, we find that human pastors are never called 'The Shepherd' but are repeatedly tasked with the verb 'to shepherd' (to 'pastor'). They are, therefore, **called to be under-shepherds**, whose entire ministry is defined by how closely they imitate the self-giving commitment of the one true Divine Shepherd.

The Under-Shepherd in Scripture

The Bible often employs the metaphor of the shepherd to describe the role of spiritual leaders, holding them to the standard of care set by the Father (the Great Shepherd), the Son (the Good and Chief Shepherd), and the Holy Spirit (the Indwelling Guide).

In the New Testament, the Greek word for "pastor" is the same as the word for "shepherd" (poimen).

Here are key scriptures where pastors or church leaders (referred to as "elders" or "overseers") are likened to shepherds:

New Testament
- **Ephesians 4:11**

"And He Himself gave some to be apostles, some prophets, some evangelists, and some pastors and teachers..."

(Note: As stated above, the word poimen - translated as "pastor" there literally means "shepherd").
- **Acts 20:28** (Paul's address to the elders of Ephesus)

"Therefore take heed to yourselves and to all the flock, among which the Holy Spirit has made you overseers, to shepherd the church of God which He purchased with His own blood."

- **1 Peter 5:1-4** (Peter's exhortation to the elders)

"Shepherd the flock of God which is among you, serving as overseers, not by compulsion but willingly, not for dishonest gain but eagerly; nor as being lords over those entrusted to you, but being examples to the flock; and when the Chief Shepherd appears, you will receive the unfading crown of glory."

- **John 21:15-17** (Jesus' charge to Peter)

15 So when they had eaten breakfast, Jesus said to Simon Peter, "Simon, son of Jonah, do you love Me more than these?"

He said to Him, "Yes, Lord; You know that I love You."

He said to him, "Feed My lambs."

16 He said to him again a second time, "Simon, son of Jonah, do you love Me?"

He said to Him, "Yes, Lord; You know that I love You."

He said to him, "Tend My sheep."

17 He said to him the third time, "Simon, son of Jonah, do you love Me?" Peter was grieved because He said to him the third time, "Do you love Me?" And he said to Him, "Lord, You know all things; You know that I love You."

Jesus said to him, "Feed My sheep.

Jesus instructs Peter with three commands to care for His people, using shepherding terms:
- "Feed My lambs."
- "Tend My sheep."
- "Feed My sheep."

Old Testament (Prophetic Warning and Promise to Leaders/Shepherds of Israel)

The Old Testament often uses the term "shepherd" for kings and national leaders, which serves as a foundation for the New Testament's application to spiritual leaders. These passages often condemn unfaithful leaders while promising to send righteous ones.[iv]
- **Jeremiah 3:15** (Promise of faithful leadership)

"And I will give you shepherds according to My heart, who will feed you with knowledge and understanding."

- **Jeremiah 23:1-4** (Condemnation of wicked leaders/shepherds)

"Woe to the shepherds who destroy and scatter the sheep of My pasture!" declares the Lord... I will set up shepherds over them who will feed them; and they shall fear no more, nor be dismayed, nor shall they be lacking," says the Lord.

- **Ezekiel 34:2** (Prophecy against false shepherds)

"Son of man, prophesy against the shepherds of Israel, prophesy and say to them, even to the shepherds, 'Thus says the Lord God: Woe to the

shepherds of Israel who feed themselves! Should not the shepherds feed the flock?'"

Shepherding, at its core, sets forth the biblical model for Christian fatherhood. Following the examples of the Heavenly Father, Jesus Christ, and faithful pastors, **earthly fathers are called to shepherd their families.**

Questions for Reflection and Discussion

The Under-Shepherd's Mandate: Imitating Christ

- **The Standard of Imitation:** Human pastors are called to 'shepherd' (a verb), constantly seeking to imitate the Divine Shepherd. As a father, what are one or two practical ways you can more closely **imitate** Christ's self-giving commitment in your family's daily life this week?

- **Shepherding vs. Lordship (1 Peter 5:3):** Peter warns leaders against **"being lords over those entrusted to you"** but instead being **"examples to the flock."**

  - In your home, do you lead by **example** (showing your children how to live out faith, handle stress, treat others) or do you attempt to **dominate** (use power and position to compel behavior without modeling it)?

  - *For Discussion:* What does genuine, humble **shepherding** look like in a conflict with your spouse or child, compared to "lordship"?

- **The Chief Shepherd's Appearance (1 Peter 5:4):** Pastors are exhorted to serve faithfully, anticipating the reward from the **Chief Shepherd**. Does the awareness that you will give an account to God for the care of your family motivate you? If so, what is the single most important change you need to make in your fathering *right now* in light of this accountability?

The Three Commands: Feed, Tend, and Feed Again

- **The Mandate to Feed (John 21:15, 17):** Jesus commands Peter, **"Feed My lambs"** and **"Feed My sheep."**

    - What is the **spiritual diet** you are primarily providing for your family (Bible, devotionals, church attendance, character lessons)? Is the food **nourishing** (knowledge and understanding, Jeremiah 3:15) or are they primarily feeding on **junk food** (frivolous media, shallow concerns)?

    - *For Reflection:* Are you tailoring the spiritual food to the age and stage of your children (**lambs** vs. **sheep**)?

- **The Mandate to Tend (John 21:16):** Jesus also commands Peter to **"Tend My sheep,"** focusing on hands-on care and management. Beyond feeding, what does it mean for you to **'tend'** to the social, emotional, and mental health of your children? Identify one area where a child needs your **active attention and hands-on care** this week.

- **Purchased with Blood (Acts 20:28):** Paul reminds the elders that the Church was purchased with Christ's blood. Though your family is your biological heritage, they are spiritually **God's possession**. How does the knowledge that your family's ultimate worth was paid for by the **blood of Christ** influence the patience and reverence with which you treat them?

The Warning of False Shepherds (The Negative Example)

- **Feeding Themselves (Ezekiel 34:2):** The prophet condemns shepherds who **"feed themselves"** while neglecting the flock. In your role as a father, are you prioritizing your own comfort, ambition, and personal desires **(feeding yourself)** over the immediate needs and nurture of your family?

- **Destroy and Scatter (Jeremiah 23:1):** Wicked shepherds **"destroy and scatter the sheep."** What decisions or attitudes in your life might inadvertently be **scattering** your family (e.g., constant travel, emotional withdrawal, inconsistency, unresolved anger)? What is one thing you can do to actively **gather** your family this week?

- **The Prophetic Parallel:** The Old Testament used the term 'shepherd' for kings and national leaders. In the daily 'kingdom' of your home, are you serving as the kind of faithful, humble leader that God has promised to provide?

CHAPTER 7
Earthly Fathers as Shepherds

The Ministry of Provision, Protection, and Guidance

Fathers are called to the essential ministry of shepherding their families. This role requires mirroring the protective, sacrificial, and guiding love exemplified by God (the Great Shepherd), Jesus (the Good/Chief Shepherd), and spiritual leaders (the under-shepherds).

The essence of a father's shepherding is built upon four non-negotiable duties.

1. Provision and Sustenance: Creating the Green Pastures

The shepherd ensures the flock lacks nothing, leading them to environments that promote life and rest (Psalm 23:1-2). A father's provision extends far beyond financial means; it is about creating a stable, nurtured life.[v]

- **Physical Provision:** This is the baseline duty: working diligently to provide food, shelter, and material security for the family.

- **Spiritual Sustenance (Still Waters):** Just as God guides us to life-giving truth, the father must be the primary source of spiritual nourishment. This means leading the family in prayer, reading and discussing Scripture, and modeling genuine faith, leading them beside the "still waters" of truth and peace (Deuteronomy 6:6-7).

- **Emotional Provision (Green Pastures):** The shepherd creates a place of rest where the sheep can lie down safely and securely. A father's duty is to ensure the home is a haven of peace and stability — a Green Pasture free from chaos, fear, and hostility. His commitment to loving his wife (Ephesians 5:25) is the foundation of this security for the children.

2. Protection and Sacrifice: The Rod Against the Wolf

Jesus established the highest standard by being the Good Shepherd who lays down His life for the sheep (John 10:11). A father's love must be sacrificial, placing the family's security above his own comfort.

- **Sacrificial Presence:** Protection begins not with a grand act, but with the daily sacrifice of time and attention. Shepherding is not delegation; it is presence. A father lays down his life by **giving up personal pursuits** to be present, engaged, and focused on his children.

- **Guarding Against the Wolves:** A father serves as the spiritual gatekeeper and defender (The Rod). This requires active vigilance, not passive observation, against the "wolves" that threaten a child's innocence and future:

    - Harmful media and online predators (pornography and other destructive content).

    - Destructive peer influence and cultural pressures (online and real life).

- Addictive or ruinous habits (gambling, substance abuse, etc).

- **Shepherding in Crisis (The Valley):** The most profound comfort of Psalm 23 is knowing the Shepherd is present in the "valley of the shadow of death" (Psalm 23:4). A father must be the family's rock through loss, fear, and suffering, modeling resilience and directing the family's hope toward God.

In Part 2, we will dive deeper into leading the family through the Valley of the Shadow of Death.

3. Guidance and Correction: The Staff of Wisdom

Pastors are called to shepherd (the verb) by leading the flock, modeling faith, and restoring those who have strayed. In much the same way, a father is the children's primary shepherd, reflecting the guidance of Christ.

- **Leading by Example (The Path):** The shepherd walks ahead of the flock, and the sheep follow. A father's personal integrity and humility are the most potent forms of guidance. His children are watching his work ethic, his treatment of his wife, and his own devotion to God — this is the path they will follow (1 Peter 5:3).

- **Intimate Knowledge and Accountability:** Just as Jesus knows His sheep by name, a father must know his children intimately — their struggles, their gifts, and their "spiritual temperature" (John 10:14). This intimate knowledge is essential for effective guidance.

- **Redemptive Correction (The Staff):** The shepherd uses the hook of his staff to
  pull a straying sheep back to safety; he does not use it to beat them. A father's correction must be redemptive, aimed at restoring the child to the right path (Proverbs 29:15). This loving correction establishes clear boundaries — the Comfort of the Rod and Staff — which are an expression of care and security, not anger.

- **Seeking the Lost:** If a child strays, the father must actively pursue, call, and restore that child, demonstrating the unconditional love of God the Father while patiently seeking their return and repentance.

The earthly father, in his role as a spiritual shepherd to his family, derives his authority and capacity solely from his submission to the Triune God. To lead his family effectively, his own life must be one of discipleship and humility under authority.

4. The Father Must Follow Christ

The father's leadership must be a faithful reflection of Christ, the Good Shepherd. He cannot guide his family where he is unwilling to walk himself. His primary duty is to model genuine discipleship, defined by submission to the Lord. His moral authority is validated by the humility of his own obedience, allowing him to authentically echo the Apostle's instruction: **"Follow me as I follow Christ"** (1 Corinthians 11:1).

The Father Must Yield to the Leading of the Holy Spirit

A godly father must first be a follower, ensuring his decisions and direction for his children are rooted in divine wisdom, not personal impulse. By actively **yielding to the leading of the Holy Spirit**, he secures the internal guidance necessary to maintain the "paths of righteousness" (Psalm 23:3), correcting with grace and teaching with spiritual authority.

The Father Must Submit to Appointed Church Leadership

The father must model for his family the importance of submission to spiritual covering as he submits to the human "under-shepherds" God has given to the Church — apostles, prophets, evangelists, pastors (shepherds), and teachers.[vi] A father's **willing submission to his spiritual leaders** demonstrates the principle of spiritual accountability. It secures a vital layer of support and oversight for his family's spiritual well-being. This leadership was established by God to "**keep watch over your souls, as those who must give an account**" (Hebrews 13:17), ensuring the father and his family remain securely in the broader fold of God's people.

Leading to the Chief Shepherd

A father is an **imperfect, temporary under-shepherd**. His entire ministry is measured by how effectively he leads his family to the one source of perfect provision and eternal security: Jesus Christ, the Chief Shepherd (1 Peter 5:4).

His goal is not to keep the sheep for himself, but to ultimately guide them to the feet of the Great Shepherd who will welcome them into the eternal Father's house.

Team Shepherding

For all of the above, the Divine Designer of the family intended every child to have both a father and a mother operating in love and within a marriage covenant as a parenting team (**Genesis 2:24, Matthew 19:4-6**). Working together, they supply guidance, protection, and provision, as two is better than one (**Ecclesiastes 4:9**).

This design reflects the communal nature of God Himself and serves as the primary vessel for discipleship, as parents are commanded to diligently teach their children the ways of the Lord (**Deuteronomy 6:6-7**).

Questions for Reflection and Discussion

1. Provision and Sustenance: Creating the Green Pastures

- **Beyond Financial Provision:** The father's duty is to create a stable, nurtured life. Besides paying the bills, what is one tangible way you actively ensure your family is **spiritually nourished** (through leading prayer, reading Scripture, etc.)?

- **Home as a Green Pasture:** A Green Pasture is a place of rest, security, and stability. How would your wife and children currently rate the **emotional atmosphere** of your home? Is it a true **haven** of peace and safety, or is it frequently disturbed by chaos, hostility, or your own unmanaged stress?

- **The Foundation of Security:** The father's commitment to loving his wife is the foundation of the children's security. In what specific, demonstrable ways are you loving your wife/co-parent **today** so that your children can **"lie down safely"** in the "green pastures" of your home?

2. Protection and Sacrifice: The Rod Against the Wolf

- **Sacrificial Presence:** Protection begins with the daily sacrifice of time and attention. Name one personal pursuit (a hobby, extra screen time, excessive work) that you are willing to **lay down** this week to ensure you are **present, engaged, and focused** on your family.

- **Guarding Against the Wolves:** A father serves as the active spiritual gatekeeper (The Rod). What is one specific **"wolf"** (harmful media, destructive content, bad peer influence) that is currently knocking on the door of your home, and what **active, vigilant step** are you taking right now to defend against it?

- **Modeling Resilience in the Valley:** When your family walks through a "valley of the shadow of death" (loss, sickness, fear), your role is to be the rock. How effectively do you model **hope and resilience** for your children, directing their focus toward **God** rather than succumbing to fear or despair yourself?

3. Guidance and Correction: The Staff of Wisdom

- **Leading by Example (The Path):** Your personal integrity and humility are the path your children will follow. Name one area of your **personal integrity** (work ethic, honesty, self-control) that you know your children are watching closely. Are you comfortable with them following that example?

- **Redemptive Correction (The Staff):** Correction must be redemptive, aimed at restoration, not fueled by anger. When was the last time you used correction (your **Staff**) not just to stop a behavior, but to gently **pull a straying child back** to safety, demonstrating Christ-like love and security?

- **Intimate Knowledge:** Do you know the "spiritual temperature" of each of your children? What is one specific question you can ask a child **today** that moves beyond surface-level conversation to reveal their current struggles, fears, or secret gifts?

4. The Father's Submission: Modeling Discipleship

- **Following Christ:** You cannot guide your family where you are unwilling to walk. In what areas of your life (e.g., prayer, obedience, service) do you need to increase your **personal submission to Christ** so that your "Follow me as I follow Christ" instruction to your children becomes authentic?

- **Yielding to the Holy Spirit:** A godly father is first a humble follower. What is your consistent practice for **actively yielding** your decisions and parenting direction to the Holy Spirit, ensuring you correct with grace and teach with divine wisdom?

- **Submission to Spiritual Accountability:** The father must model submission to church leadership to secure a layer of spiritual oversight. What is one way you can better demonstrate to your children the importance of **spiritual accountability** by actively submitting to and honoring the "under-shepherds" God has placed over your family?

- **Leading to the Chief Shepherd:** Your ultimate goal is to lead your family to the feet of Christ. What is the single most important message or habit you want your children to take away from your fathering that will ensure they are securely in the **eternal Father's house**?

- **Co-Shepherding:** God's original design is for every child to have both a father and a mother as a parenting team. In what ways are you intentionally leading in your

marriage to build and maintain a strong parenting
partnership?

CHAPTER 8
Shepherds Approved and Disapproved by God

Not all shepherding is the same, because not all shepherds are equal. Most shepherds in the ancient Middle East were not the owners of the sheep they tended; they were often either family members of the owner (like a son) or hired hands (also called hirelings).

This distinction is central to the Biblical metaphor of the shepherd.

Types of Shepherds and the Father Analogy

In the context of biblical shepherding, there were two primary categories, and the level of care was directly tied to the level of ownership and commitment:

Type 1. The Owner/Family Shepherd (The Human Father)

This shepherd either owned the flock outright or was the son/daughter of the owner (e.g., David tending his father Jesse's flock, or Moses tending Jethro's flock).

- **Motivation: Love, legacy, and personal stake.** They have an intrinsic investment in the welfare of every single animal.

- **Action:** The work of the owner/family shepherd is characterized by **sacrificial commitment.** They know the sheep by name and are willing to risk their lives to protect the flock.

- **Father Analogy:** This is the ideal model for a human father. A father's "flock" (his children) is his own (to steward for God, the ultimate Owner); his commitment is based on **love**, not wages. His leadership is **sacrificial**, like Jesus, the **Good Shepherd**, who lays down his life for the sheep (John 10:11).

Type 2. The Hired Hand or Hireling (The Non-Committed)

This shepherd was an employee who received a wage to watch the sheep, often considered a low-status job.

- **Motivation: Wages, duty, and self-preservation.** Their low-wage contracts limit their concern for the flock.

- **Action:** As Jesus notes, when the wolf comes, the hireling "abandons the sheep and runs away because he is a hired hand and cares nothing for the sheep" (John 10:12-13). They are **unreliable** in a crisis.

- **Father Analogy:** This is the danger zone for fathers. A father who is physically or emotionally **absent**, or whose commitment is based on convenience, acts like a hireling. His commitment vanishes when the "wolf" (crisis, addiction, financial hardship, relationship difficulties, distractions of various kinds) attacks.

The metaphor is powerful precisely because Jesus explicitly rejects the hireling model. He approves authentic, committed leadership, contending that genuine care stems only from ownership and sacrificial love.

The Tragedy of Shepherdless Sheep: America's Fatherlessness Crisis

The spiritual crisis of "sheep without a shepherd," abandoned by hirelings who cared only for themselves, finds a chilling contemporary parallel in the **fatherlessness crisis** gripping America. Today, millions of children — nearly **one in four** — grow up without a biological, step, or adoptive father in the home.

The situation is worse for minority children. The approximate percentage of Black/African American children is 47% to 50%. For Hispanic/Latino children, it is 28% to 31%.

This absence creates a vacuum of guidance, protection, and provision, mirroring the ancient flock left vulnerable to wolves.

The "hireling" shepherd, who flees when danger approaches because the sheep are not his own, is tragically embodied by the absent father who has, for whatever reason, chosen to disengage. Whether the father is physically gone or merely **emotionally detached**, the result for the child is the same: a profound sense of abandonment and insecurity.

Consequences of an Absent Guide

The consequences of this familial abandonment for children's well-being are devastating and widely documented. Studies show that fatherless children are at a significantly higher risk for poverty, delinquency, substance abuse, and behavioral disorders.

Boys, lacking a masculine role model to guide their transition into responsible adulthood, may seek a sense of belonging and structure in **"toxic substitutes"** like gangs, becoming the very "wolves" the good shepherd protects against. Girls, missing the consistent affirmation of a loving father, often struggle with low self-esteem and a more profound vulnerability to unhealthy relationships.

The father, like a faithful shepherd, is meant to be a source of strength, identity, and direction; his absence leaves the young with a lifelong struggle to find their way. The crisis of the absent father is, in essence, the ultimate tragedy of shepherdless sheep — a generation left to wander an increasingly dangerous social landscape without their primary guide and protector.

Why So Much Father Absence?

The absence of a father in the home is rarely due to a single cause but stems from a complex interplay of personal choices, social upheaval, parental alienation, and economic pressures.

These factors collectively contribute to the modern "hireling" syndrome, where the primary caregiver abandons, neglects, or is prevented from fulfilling their role.

Personal and Behavioral Factors

- **Lack of Commitment/Paternal Maturity:** A fundamental failure to grasp the **sacrificial, long-term nature of fatherhood**. This includes a reluctance to transition from a focus on self-interest and personal freedom to a commitment to the child's well-being.

- **Addictions and Substance Abuse:** Chronic dependency on drugs, alcohol, or other self-destructive behaviors that lead to emotional unavailability, financial ruin, and an inability to function responsibly as a parent.

- **Emotional Detachment ("Present Absenteeism"):** Even when physically present, a father may be **emotionally distant** or unavailable due to preoccupation with technology, work, or hobbies, resulting in a weak or unformed bond with the child.

- **Intergenerational Cycle of Absence:** Fathers who grew up without an engaged father often lack a blueprint or positive model for raising their own children, perpetuating the cycle of fatherlessness.

Societal and Economic Factors

- **Divorce and Family Breakdown:** High rates of divorce and the subsequent complexities of custody arrangements often result in a father's reduced or eliminated involvement in the child's daily life, especially over time.

- **Non-Marital Births:** The sharp increase in children born to unmarried mothers, where the initial paternal bond or commitment is often tenuous or nonexistent from the start.

- **Incarceration:** High rates of male incarceration physically remove fathers from the home for extended periods, severing ties and contributing to economic instability.

- **Economic Strain and Work Culture:** The pressure to work **multiple jobs or extremely long hours** to provide financially can lead to a practical absence, prioritizing provision over presence. While often intended as an act of love, this imbalance still results in emotional distance from the children.

- **Cultural Shift:** A societal devaluation of marriage and stable family units, coupled with cultural messages that minimize the **unique and irreplaceable role of the father** in a child's psychological and moral development.

- **Maternal Gatekeeping:** Other fathers, who are often the noncustodial parents, struggle to spend time with their children due to the mother's "gatekeeping." A gatekeeper parent limits the other parent's involvement in the child's life, causing pain, frustration, sadness, and anger for the father, who must ask permission to see his kids and is often denied access.

- **Parental Alienation:** This is a complex psychological process where one parent manipulates a child into rejecting or resenting the other parent. Parental alienation can have devastating effects on children, causing emotional distress, anxiety, and even long-term psychological damage. It can also disrupt the child's relationship with the alienated parent, leading to feelings of guilt, confusion, and resentment.

These diverse reasons reveal that the crisis of the absent father is not merely a personal failing but a symptom of profound societal and moral disorientation, making the children truly "sheep without a shepherd" in a challenging world. Society should place a higher priority on addressing this catastrophe for the sake of the children.

Being physically present alone is not enough, however. **Shepherding well requires full presence – body, mind, soul, and spirit.**

Questions for Reflection and Discussion

Types of Shepherds and the Father Analogy

- **The Owner's Motivation:** The Owner/Family Shepherd is motivated by **love, legacy, and personal stake**. As a father, how often do you approach the challenges of parenting from a place of **personal, intrinsic investment** (love and legacy), versus merely fulfilling a reluctant duty (a "hireling" mindset)?

- **Sacrificial Commitment:** The Owner Shepherd is willing to risk his life; the Hireling **"abandons the sheep and runs away"** when the wolf comes. Identify a current **"wolf"** (a crisis, a long-term challenge, a strong distraction) attacking your family right now. Are you leaning into it with **sacrificial commitment** or are you tempted to mentally or emotionally **flee** from the difficulty?

- **"Cares Nothing for the Sheep":** Jesus' judgment of the hireling is stark: he **"cares nothing for the sheep."** How does this powerful phrase challenge you regarding areas of "present absenteeism" where you may be physically present but **emotionally detached** (preoccupied with work, technology, or hobbies)?

The Tragedy of Shepherdless Sheep

- **The Fatherlessness Crisis:** The chapter states that nearly **one in four** children in America grow up without a father in the home, with rates significantly higher for minority children (e.g., approximately **47-50%** for Black/African American children).

o If you grew up without an engaged father, how are you actively working to **break the intergenerational cycle** and build a positive blueprint for your children that you never received?

o If you are a father who is physically present, what specific, non-negotiable step can you take this week to ensure your children never feel the devastating effects of **emotional absence**?

- **Consequences of an Absent Guide:** The absent father leaves a vacuum that leads boys to seek "**toxic substitutes**" and leaves girls vulnerable to **unhealthy relationships**. As a shepherd, what are you intentionally doing **today** to fill your children's lives with a strong sense of **identity, affirmation, and belonging** so they do not seek destructive substitutes?

- **Physical vs. Emotional Absence:** The chapter notes that the result for the child is the same whether the father is physically gone or merely emotionally detached. How can you increase your **full presence**—body, mind, soul, and spirit—in your interactions with your children over the next 48 hours?

Why So Much Father Absence? (The Hireling Syndrome)

- **Prioritizing Presence over Provision:** Economic strain often leads to fathers prioritizing work (provision) over presence. How can you adjust your schedule or priorities to ensure you are meeting the need for **both** provision and active presence without sacrificing one for the other?

- **Navigating Alienation and Gatekeeping:** For fathers who are noncustodial parents: If you face maternal gatekeeping or parental alienation, how can you consistently demonstrate **unwavering, patient love** and pursuit of your children, modeling the relentless pursuit of the Good Shepherd, even when access is painful and frustrating?

- **The Cultural Shift:** If society devalues the unique role of the father, how will you counteract that message within your home by consistently **affirming and demonstrating** the irreplaceable importance of a faithful father's leadership and protection?

CHAPTER 9
The Shepherd's Presence: Fully Engaged in Guiding Your Flock

A shepherd who is inattentive, wandering, or distracted cannot effectively guide his sheep. This chapter is an invitation to make a profound commitment to being fully present—to live, work, and guide your family through every type of terrain with intimate engagement. We will explore the concept of the shepherd's presence and provide actionable tips you can begin practicing today, even in the valleys.

Tending the Flock: Making and Maintaining Mindful Connection

For the father-shepherd, **being fully present** isn't just about being in the same house; it's about stepping into the grazing field of your child's world with your **entire focus**. It is the attentive shepherd's vigilant watchfulness that ensures the flock's safety and well-being.

To be truly present, the shepherd must put away the world's distractions, silence the clamor of personal concerns, and **tune in** to the needs of his sheep. This involves **listening** not just to the sounds of their words, but also to the unspoken language of their fears, frustrations, and triumphs. The attentive shepherd responds with **empathy**, validating their emotions, and mirroring their excitement—letting them know that their feelings are safe within the fold.

It is in these moments of **mindful connection** that you build the bridge of trust necessary for effective leadership. This is how the shepherd shows his flock that they are **seen, heard, and valued**. You become a **safe harbor**, a constant presence of love and support in their ever-expanding, sometimes frightening, world. This intimacy, once established, is the shepherd's most precious resource and must be fiercely protected from anything that would cause distraction or distance.

The Danger of the Wandering Shepherd

Imagine a shepherd tending his flock while gazing at something far off, or while absorbed in an activity that makes him oblivious to the wolves circling the edges of the field.

In the physical world, we have laws against **distracted driving** because we recognize that a moment's inattention can lead to disaster. As the shepherd of your family, you face a similar, though far more subtle, danger: **distracted parenting**. While there are no legal statutes against a mentally, emotionally, or spiritually wandering shepherd, the consequences are real and severe.

Just as a shepherd's lack of focus can lead to immediate harm to his flock, a family shepherd's failure to be fully present also has consequences, often more subtle than a physical accident. The effects are a **slow erosion of trust and connection**.

For instance, when a family shepherd is distracted by browsing social media, watching video reels, excessive TV, or personal gaming, his attention is stolen from the most critical responsibility he has: the careful, nurturing guidance of his children. Other distractions — such as sports fanaticism, gambling, alcoholism, and other addictions — are predators that consume the shepherd's focus and effectively communicate to his children that their **needs are secondary** to the father's pursuits.

The Consequences of the Partially Present Shepherd

Over time, a failure to be fully present with a child can fracture the father-child bond, ultimately weakening the entire family. The shepherd's indifference leaves the sheep vulnerable, both to external threats and internal difficulties.

Vulnerabilities for the Sheep (The Child):

- **Difficulty with Emotional Regulation:** Sheep without the constant, secure presence of their shepherd struggle to maintain peace in the field. A child may react to stress with emotional outbursts or withdrawal, lacking the safe base to process their feelings.

- **Social Difficulties and Low Trust:** Feeling emotionally distant from their guide, they may struggle to form healthy relationships or trust others outside their immediate family.

- **Weakened Self-Worth:** The perceived neglect tells the sheep they are not important enough to command the shepherd's full attention, negatively impacting self-esteem.

Cost to the Shepherd (The Father):

- **Missed Opportunities:** The distracted shepherd misses the unique joys and profound rewards of guiding his children through their lives' milestones, both big and small.

- **Regret and Lost Influence:** The resulting lack of closeness leads to feelings of regret and frustration, and crucially, strips the father of the trust required to truly influence and guide his children when they need it most.

- **Tension in the Fold:** The shepherd's unavailability creates imbalance and tension within the family unit, leaving the entire flock feeling insecure.

Our focus is on equipping you to be an **attentive and engaged shepherd**, building the strong, secure bond necessary for the welfare and healthy development of your family.

Maximizing the Shepherd's Presence

Being a fully present shepherd is a practiced discipline, not a passive state of being. These tips are the essential tools for removing barriers and maximizing your time in the fold.

Action: Fence Off Distractions

When a sheep bleats for your attention, the shepherd acknowledges it immediately. Taking the following steps **fences off** the distractions and sends this unmistakable message: **"You are my priority. I am here to listen."**

1. **Stop scrolling and put down the phone—screen down.** The communication device that connects you to the world is the **primary wolf** that steals your presence. Set it aside.

2. **Turn off the TV and/or game system.** These distractions divide your attention, making you a **half-shepherd**. Dedicate your eyes and ears entirely to your child.

3. **Close the magazine or book.** Your reading material will wait. The opportunity to connect with your child **will not**.

This conscious choice to be fully "present" is the most meaningful **gift** you can give your flock. If you are new to this practice, your older children may be wary. Be **patient and consistent**. Your faithfulness in this small discipline will strengthen your bond and open a deep channel of communication for life-long guidance.

Practice Attentive Listening: Hearing the Shepherd's Call

Effective guidance begins not with speaking, but with listening.

1. **Maintain Eye-to-Eye Contact.** Face your child in a relaxed, non-confrontational posture. For younger lambs, this may mean getting on the floor to meet them at their level.

2. **Tune In to Them.** This requires consciously **tuning out** the mental noise of your own life. You must focus your entire inner attention on their voice, just as a shepherd listens for the faintest cry of a lost lamb.

3. **Practice Non-Judgmental Listening.** While children are talking:

- **Fully listen** to understand. Do not interrupt, interpret, or assign a motive.

- **Withhold judgment.** You are gathering facts and feelings first.

- **Avoid formulating a response.** Your primary task is to understand, not to advise.

4. **Provide Feedback for Clarification.** This shows your deep engagement.

- "So, what I hear you saying is… "

- "Really? You mean… ?"

5. **Ask Open-Ended Questions to Keep the Communication Open.**

- "That is interesting! Can you tell me more about that?"

- "How did that make you feel?"

- "What do you plan to do about that?"

- "How can I help?"

These techniques ensure that when you finally offer your words of wisdom, counsel, or correction, your child is open to receiving them because they trust that their **shepherd is fully present** and genuinely cares.

The Shepherd's Indifference vs. The Shepherd's Discipline

The Scriptures provide a direct charge to the father-shepherd:

"Fathers, do not provoke your children to anger [do not exasperate them to the point of resentment with demands that are trivial or unreasonable or humiliating or abusive; nor by showing favoritism or **indifference** to any of them], but bring them up [tenderly, with lovingkindness] in the **discipline and instruction of the Lord.**" - Ephesians 6:4 (Amplified Bible)

The **indifference** warned against is the very antithesis of presence. An indifferent father is a shepherd who neglects his flock, allowing his children to feel undervalued, which provokes anger and resentment in them. The call to be present is a call to **tenderness, loving kindness**, ensuring that all guidance—the discipline and instruction of the Lord—is delivered from a place of deep, undeniable, and **fully present** love.

Questions for Reflection and Discussion

Tending the Flock: Making and Maintaining Mindful Connection

- **Defining Presence:** The chapter defines presence as stepping into your child's world with your **entire focus**. How often do you make and maintain **mindful connection** with your children (fully focused on them)? Be honest: Does your child currently perceive you as a "safe harbor," or as a figure who is easily distracted or emotionally distant?

- **The Unspoken Language:** The shepherd listens not just to the sounds of their words, but also to the **unspoken language** of their fears and frustrations. Name one child in your life right now. Based on their behavior this week, what is the **unspoken fear** or frustration that you need to "tune in" to and address?

- **The Bridge of Trust:** Mindful connection builds the **bridge of trust** necessary for effective leadership. Reflect on a recent interaction where your distraction or pre-occupation hindered your ability to connect with your child. What was the **cost** of that missed opportunity?

The Danger of the Wandering Shepherd

- **The Primary Wolf:** The chapter identifies the communication device (phone, scrolling, gaming) as the **primary wolf** that steals your presence.

o   What is your family's current **rule or boundary** for technology and media consumption, and how faithfully are *you* adhering to it?

o   What is the practical step you can take today to **"fence off"** a key distraction (put the phone away, turn off the game) for a specific, dedicated block of time with your family?

- **Present Absenteeism:** "Present Absenteeism" (physical presence without emotional engagement) is a subtle danger that erodes trust. In what ways might your current work habits, hobbies, or personal pursuits be unknowingly communicating to your children that their needs are **secondary** to your self-interest?

Consequences and Maximizing Presence

- **The Shepherd's Indifference (Ephesians 6:4):** The Scripture warns against indifference, which provokes **anger and resentment** in children. When was the last time a child's frustration or emotional outburst was a symptom of feeling **undervalued or ignored** by you, the shepherd, rather than simple rebellion?

- **Redeeming Lost Influence:** The failure to be present strips the father of the **trust required to truly influence** his children when they need it most. If you sense a decline in your influence with an older child, how might a renewed commitment to **attentive listening** and **consistent presence** be the first step in restoring that influence?

- **Practicing Attentive Listening:** The discipline of active listening requires a commitment to non-judgmental attention.

  - Which of the **Attentive Listening Tips** (e.g., maintain eye-to-eye contact, avoid formulating a response, ask open-ended questions) is the hardest for you to practice, and why?

  - Commit to using one clarifying phrase, such as, **"So, what I hear you saying is..."** in a meaningful conversation with your child this week to ensure they feel truly **heard and valued**.

What is the greatest threat to your presence with your children right now, and what is one concrete step you will take this week to remove that distraction from the fold?

CHAPTER10
The Blessings and Rewards of Shepherding Well

The Bible indicates that the blessings and rewards of shepherding (parenting) children well are primarily rooted in spiritual continuity, social honor, personal peace, and future security.

These rewards are presented not merely as temporal payments, but as the natural, God-ordained fruit of faithful diligence.

Wisdom and Joy in the Present

The most immediate blessings are the emotional and spiritual rewards that parents themselves enjoy.

- **Joy and Delight:** A well-guided child brings pleasure and alleviates stress. Proverbs repeatedly emphasizes this: *"A wise son makes a glad father"* (Proverbs 10:1) and *"The father of a righteous man will greatly rejoice; he who fathers a wise son will be glad in him"* (Proverbs 23:24).

- **Rest from Shame:** Successful parenting guards the parent's reputation and peace of mind. *"Correct your son, and he will give you rest; yes, he will give delight to your soul"* (Proverbs 29:17). Conversely, a child who is not shepherded well brings *"grief and shame"* (Proverbs 19:26).

- **Personal Blessing:** The diligence of a parent is blessed. The shepherd/parent who cares for his own "flock" will receive the finest of the harvest: *"He who tends the fig tree will eat its fruit, and he who guards his master will be honored"* (Proverbs 27:18).

Stability and Security in the Future

The Bible presents children as a heritage and a strategic resource, giving parents confidence later in life.

- **A Mighty Heritage:** Children are a tremendous blessing from God. *"Behold, children are a heritage from the LORD, the fruit of the womb a reward"* (Psalm 127:3).

- **Defense and Advocacy (The Arrow Metaphor):** Righteous children are compared to arrows in a warrior's hand, defending the parents' interests in public or later life: *"Like arrows in the hand of a warrior, so are the children of one's youth. Happy is the man who has his quiver full of them; they shall not be put to shame when they speak with their enemies in the gate"* (Psalm 127:4-5). This speaks to honor and security in public life.

- **Comfort in Old Age:** Shepherded children are expected to honor and care for their parents, ensuring their parents are not abandoned in their final years (Proverbs 23:22).

Spiritual Continuity and Eternal Impact

The greatest reward is the fulfillment of the covenant—seeing the legacy of faith continue and multiply.

- **Covenant Fulfillment:** The Old Testament promises that God's people would teach their children to love and obey God (Deuteronomy 6:6-7). The reward is the continuity of faith across generations. *"The blessing of the LORD is on the house of the righteous"* (Proverbs 3:33).

- **Fruit for the Harvest:** The reward aligns with the mission of the Chief Shepherd (Jesus Christ). When parents raise children who follow Christ, they are contributing to the eternal "flock," resulting in a reward from the Chief Shepherd Himself. This future reward is ultimately a share in the glory of the eternal Kingdom (1 Peter 5:4).

- **Exaltation:** The ultimate reward is a share in the joy of God, who is the Father/Shepherd who desires all His children to be restored and saved.

Questions for Reflection and Discussion

Wisdom and Joy in the Present

- **The Glad Father (Proverbs 10:1):** The Bible links a child's wisdom directly to the father's **joy and gladness**. When you consider the life of your children today, what specific choices or character traits in them bring you the deepest sense of delight and fulfillment as a father?

- **Rest from Shame (Proverbs 29:17):** Faithful shepherding is promised to bring the father **rest from shame** and **delight to his soul**. What emotional or mental "rest" do you currently enjoy because you have been diligent in correcting and guiding your children? Conversely, what current source of worry or lack of peace is a direct result of guidance you know you have neglected?

- **Eating the Fruit of the Fig Tree (Proverbs 27:18):** This verse promises that the diligent shepherd/parent will **"eat its fruit."** What are the tangible, short-term "fruits" (positive experiences, healthy relationships, family harmony) you are currently enjoying because of the consistent time and effort you have invested in your family this past year?

Stability and Security in the Future

- **The Arrow Metaphor (Psalm 127:4-5):** Righteous children are like **arrows** that provide **defense and advocacy** in later life.

    o What are you doing today to "sharpen your arrows" (train your children in truth, integrity, and competence) so they can stand strong and speak effectively on your behalf and the family's behalf in the public square?

○ *For Discussion:* How do you model handling "enemies in the gate" (conflict, public disagreement, criticism) so that your children learn to be courageous and honorable advocates?

- **Comfort in Old Age:** Shepherded children are expected to **honor and care** for their parents. Are you prioritizing the long-term goal of building a respectful, honoring relationship with your children, or are you sacrificing future honor for immediate peace or convenience in your parenting decisions?

- **A Heritage from the LORD (Psalm 127:3):** Children are a **heritage** and a **reward**. Does your daily interaction with your children reflect the high value God places on them as a precious gift?

Spiritual Continuity and Eternal Impact

- **Covenant Fulfillment (Deuteronomy 6:6-7):** The greatest reward is seeing the **legacy of faith continue** across generations. What is the one non-negotiable spiritual discipline you are modeling and teaching your children that you pray will still be active in their lives when they are old?

- **Fruit for the Chief Shepherd:** The ultimate reward aligns with the Chief Shepherd's mission. If you stood before Christ today, what is the single most important **spiritual fruit** in your children's lives that you would joyfully present to Him as a result of your faithful shepherding?

- **Exaltation (1 Peter 5:4):** The reward is the **unfading crown of glory.** How does the certainty of an eternal reward motivate you to endure the current, unseen, and often exhausting sacrifices of faithful fatherhood?

SECTION II

LEADING THROUGH THE VALLEYS

CHAPTER 11
The Reality of the Valley of the Shadow

In Part I, we established the father's calling: to be a loving, committed shepherd, imitating the care of the Great and Good Shepherd in **Provision, Protection, and Presence**. This noble charge, however, does not promise a life lived only on sunlit uplands and green pastures. It promises a life that, inevitably, must pass through "**The Valley of the Shadow of Death**" (Psalm 23:4).

The faithful shepherd knows these valleys are not optional detours; they are the necessary, treacherous passages through which the flock must be led.

For the sheep of ancient Israel, the valley was a literal place—a deep, dark gorge flanked by high rocks, prone to flash floods, and haunted by predators. For the father shepherding his family today, the valley is the **spiritual and emotional reality of crisis** – his children's, and his own.

Our valleys are not carved by rock and water, but by the dangers of a world hostile to innocence: the isolating lure of **pornography**, the hidden pain of **self-harm**, the frustration of **academic struggles**, the volatility of the **strong-willed child**, the pervasive threat of **online dangers** and **addictive technologies,** and so many more corrupting hazards. These are the shadowy places where the flock is most likely to scatter, fall, or be injured or taken.

Why the Shepherd Must Lead

A sheep that enters the valley alone is doomed. Its natural fear paralyzes it; its lack of vision prevents escape. The Good Shepherd does not send His sheep into the darkness; He leads them through it. This section of *The Family Shepherd* is dedicated to helping fathers emulate that Divine leadership, ensuring their presence in the valley is a source of **comfort, clarity, and courage**.

The question is not *if* your family will enter shadowy valleys, but *how* you, as their shepherd, will lead:

- **You must be Present:** The comfort is not in the absence of danger, but in the affirmation, **"You are with me"** (Psalm 23:4). The father's
  unwavering physical and emotional presence is the primary tool for combating the fear and isolation of the valley. You must be there!

- **You must use the Rod and Staff:** The valley demands the active use of the shepherd's dual tools. The **Rod** is the weapon used to fight external predators. The **Staff** is the gentle yet firm tool used to **correct and guide** the panicked or straying child and prevent them from compounding their fear with poor decisions.

- **You must maintain Vision:** While the sheep see only shadow, the shepherd knows the valley eventually opens back into sunlight and life. The father's role is to hold onto hope and guide the family with the wisdom that this dark passage, while difficult, has a purpose and a destination: **restoration and flourishing** at the other end.

- **You must practice Self-Care:** If you don't maintain your own good health, you won't have much care to give your family. The father who would shepherd well must ensure he is attending to his own physical, mental, emotional, and spiritual well-being.

Section II of *The Family Shepherd* is a practical guide for every father preparing to lead his family through both the sunlit meadows and the dark passageways. It is a call to prayerful vigilance and intervention, offering specific strategies to navigate the most dangerous passages and, ultimately, to shepherd your children safely back into the light of the Chief Shepherd.

Now, let's begin our journey of shepherding your family through some of the most treacherous terrain.

Questions for Reflection and Discussion

The Reality of the Modern Valley

- **Identifying the Valleys:** The chapter lists several modern "valleys" (pornography, self-harm, strong-willed children, online dangers).

    - Which of these, or what other specific, complex issue, currently feels like a **"shadowy passage"** or crisis affecting your child or your family's overall well-being?

    - *For Reflection:* Why is it dangerous to pretend that your family only lives on "sunlit uplands" and ignore the reality of these potential valleys?

- **The Sheep's Paralysis:** A sheep that enters the valley alone is paralyzed by **fear** and lack of **vision**. When your child is facing stress, fear, or a crisis, do they instinctively **turn toward you** for guidance, or do they retreat and try to handle the fear alone? What does their reaction tell you about the current trust level you share?

The Shepherd's Strategy in the Valley

- **The Primary Tool: Presence:** The comfort in the valley is not in the absence of danger, but in the affirmation, **"You are with me."** What is one practical, specific way you can increase your **unwavering physical and emotional presence** in your family's life this week to combat the fear and isolation they might be facing?

- **Rod and Staff in Crisis:** The valley demands the active, dual use of the **Rod** (protection/fighting external predators) and the **Staff** (gentle guidance/correction for panic).

- o When your child is spiraling into fear or poor decisions, are you able to clearly distinguish when to use the **Rod** (setting a firm boundary against danger) and when to use the **Staff** (gently correcting a panicked response)?

- o *For Discussion:* Discuss the difference between the **Rod** being used to fight the child's *behavior* versus fighting the *external predator* or temptation attacking the child.

- **Maintaining Vision (Holding Hope):** The father's role is to maintain **hope** and lead with the wisdom that the dark passage has a destination: **restoration and flourishing**. What spiritual truth or promise are you clinging to that allows you to maintain hope and speak vision into your family's crisis, even when the path is dark?

- **Prioritizing Self-Care:** The chapter emphasizes that the father must attend to his own **physical, mental, emotional, and spiritual well-being**. Name one non-negotiable, healthy practice (spiritual or physical) you will commit to this week to ensure you have the strength and clarity needed to shepherd your family through challenging terrain.

CHAPTER 12
The Dark Valley (Part 1): The Perils of Pornography

The shepherd's vigilance extends beyond the physical threats of the pasture to the silent, unseen dangers that lurk in the **dark, death-filled valleys of the 21st century.**

Today, one of the most pervasive hazards is easy, immediate access to **pornography.** While previous generations rarely encountered "dirty pictures," smartphones and high-speed internet have made this poisonous content readily available to almost anyone, anytime, anywhere. This ease of access has significantly increased exposure, especially among our young flock.

The Predator is a Powerful Industry

Based on various market research reports, recent estimates for the **global adult entertainment market** generally fall into the range of:

- **Around $58 billion to $66 billion** for recent years (like 2023 or 2024).

- Projections suggest the market could grow to around **$93 billion to over $100 billion** by the early 2030s, growing at a CAGR of around 5% to 7%[vii]

The estimated value of the **global online adult entertainment market** is a massive and rapidly growing figure, given that the internet has become the dominant platform for adult content consumption.

Their Target: Children and Youth

The Internet adult content industry targets children and youth not necessarily through explicit advertising on their own sites (which often requires age verification, however easily bypassed), but primarily through strategies that leverage mainstream online environments:

1. Cross-Platform Advertising and Content Funnels

- **Ads and Pop-ups on Non-Adult Sites:** This is one of the most common ways children are first exposed to pornography — by accidentally encountering intrusive, sexually suggestive ads or pop-ups on sites they frequent, such as **free gaming, film streaming, or sports streaming websites**.

- **Mainstream Social Media Teasers:** Adult content creators, particularly those on subscription platforms like OnlyFans, actively use platforms popular with youth (like **TikTok, Instagram, and Snapchat**) to build an audience. They post **"safe for work" or "PG-rated" content** (e.g., dance challenges, makeup tutorials, vlogs) that appears harmless to attract young followers. Their profiles then include links or "calculated funnels" leading directly to their paid, explicit adult content.

- **Influencer Marketing:** "Content houses" and individual creators on social media glamorize the adult industry lifestyle, showcasing wealth, luxury, and independence to market adult content creation as an appealing, entrepreneurial, and "empowering" career path to impressionable teenagers.

2. Accidental and Unintentional Exposure

- **Search Engines and Misspellings:** Children often stumble upon pornography unintentionally through image searches, clicking on malicious links, or simply misspelling a search term in a search engine.

- **Messaging Apps and Private Chats:** Explicit content is increasingly shared among youth themselves in private digital spaces like **group chats, Discord channels, and messaging apps** (Telegram, WhatsApp), meaning the content industry's material enters their social circles.

3. Exploitation of Algorithms and Design

- **Algorithmic Amplification:** Social media algorithms often prioritize and amplify sensational or extreme content to maximize engagement. This can result in children being fed hyper-sexualized, misogynistic, or violent content that normalizes harmful narratives.

- **Lack of Effective Age Verification:** Despite regulations and site warnings, the age-verification systems on most adult content sites are often trivial to bypass, allowing children to intentionally access material with minimal effort.

Result: Early and Widespread Exposure

Research consistently shows that the methods above are highly effective:

- The **average age of first exposure to pornography** for children is currently estimated to be around **12 to 13 years old**.

- Surveys indicate that children often encounter pornography on **social media platforms (Twitter/X, Instagram, Snapchat, TikTok)** as frequently as, or even more often than, on dedicated adult websites

Grave Hazards to the Young Flock

A child's brain is still developing, and they are not equipped to process the complex and often harmful content found in pornography. Exposure to this content at a young age can have significant and detrimental effects on the lambs in your care.[viii]

- **Distorted Views of Sexuality:** Pornography often presents unrealistic, objectifying, and exploitative depictions of sex. This can lead children to develop **skewed perceptions** of healthy sexual relationships, of consent, and of body image. It can normalize behaviors that are neither consensual nor safe.

- **Confusion and Emotional Distress:** Young minds struggle to differentiate between fantasy and reality, leading to **confusion, anxiety, and feelings of inadequacy**. The content can be emotionally overwhelming and disturbing, causing fear, sadness, and disgust.

- **Risk of Sexual Exploitation and Grooming:** Exposure to pornography can increase a child's vulnerability to sexual exploitation and abuse. Predators can use it to desensitize children to sexual acts, making it harder for the child to recognize and report abuse, and to trust their own instincts.

- **Impact on Development:** Early exposure interferes with healthy social and emotional development, affecting a child's ability to form stable, healthy relationships later in life. It can also lead to **premature sexualization**.

- **Normalization of Unhealthy Behaviors:** Pornography can normalize unhealthy behaviors, such as the objectification of individuals and the acceptance of sexual violence, causing children to believe these actions are normal and expected.

The Family Shepherd's Duty

As the father, you have the crucial, sacred responsibility to equip and protect your children. **Conversations about pornography are not optional; they are vital weapons.** The best people to have these talks with kids are their parents. Having age-appropriate, consistent discussions can help them understand the dangers and protect them from harm. The shepherd must shield his flock from this poison, recognizing it as a genuine threat to their innocence, relational capacity, and spiritual health.

Navigating the Difficult Conversation: The Shepherd's Guidance

While these are uncomfortable conversations for most of us, we must not shrink from this protective duty. Conversations about this subject should be ongoing and age-appropriate. Here are the core principles for the family shepherd:

Core Principles for the Shepherd's Discussion:

1. **Start Early and Build Gradually:** Don't wait until adolescence. Start laying the groundwork in early childhood by teaching children about body parts, appropriate touch, and **personal boundaries**. As they grow, gradually introduce more complex concepts like puberty, sexual feelings, relationships, and consent. **Consistent, ongoing conversations** are far more effective than one big, awkward talk, as they create a safe space for questions to arise naturally.

2. **Focus on Honesty and Accuracy:** Provide **honest and accurate information**, using language your child can understand. Avoid overly technical or graphic details, but **do not shy away from answering their questions truthfully**. Correct any misconceptions they may have and emphasize the clear difference between healthy sexuality (based on love and respect) and the **exploitative content** often found in pornography.

3. **Emphasize Values and Healthy Relationships:** Frame the conversation around your **family's core values and beliefs**. Focus on the importance of **respect, consent, and mutual care**. Help them understand that sex is a natural

gift from God, but it should be based on mutual respect and commitment, and that pornography **does not display healthy relationships**.

Age-Appropriate Guidance for Your Flock

Early Childhood (Preschool/Elementary)

- **Shepherd's Focus:** Body Safety and Boundaries.

- **Key Points:** Introduce **private parts** and **appropriate touch**. Teach that the body belongs to God and demands respect (1 Corinthians 6:19-20).

Middle Childhood (Pre-Teens)

- **Shepherd's Focus:** Puberty, Curiosity, and Accidental Exposure.

- **Key Points:** Discuss body changes and emerging feelings. Begin teaching **healthy relationships** and **consent**. Address device safety and the risk of accidental exposure.

Adolescence (Teens)

- **Shepherd's Focus:** Risks, Consequences, and Self-Esteem.

- **Key Points:** Discuss the **serious impact** of pornography on relationships and self-image. Provide accurate information on sex and sexuality. Stress the **absolute importance of consent and respect**.

Practical Tips for the Family Shepherd

- **Create a Safe and Open Environment:** Be the trusted, non-judgmental guide they turn to.

- **Choose the Right Time and Place:** Have these talks when you are both relaxed, free from distractions, and can give your full attention.

- **Listen Actively:** Validate your child's feelings. If they seem confused or scared, acknowledge their emotion.

- **Set Clear Boundaries and Expectations:** This is critical for **technology use.** Discuss together what is acceptable and what is off-limits.

- **Monitor Technology Use Appropriately:** The shepherd is responsible for the safety of the fold. Have systems in place that allow for responsible monitoring of devices used by minors.

Resources for the Family Shepherd

Navigating this terrain is difficult, but you don't have to do it alone. The following books are highly recommended tools for the father-shepherd:

- *Good Pictures Bad Pictures: Porn-Proofing Today's Young Kids* by **Kristen Jenson:** Excellent for laying a foundation of knowledge for younger children (ages 6-11), using simple analogies to explain the difference between appropriate and harmful content.

- *It's Time to Talk to Your Kids About Porn* by **Greta Eskridge:** Provides guidance on having honest, age-appropriate conversations for children of all ages, emphasizing **sexual integrity** and healthy relationships.

- *Every Parent's Battle: A Family Guide to Resisting Pornography*: Offers guidance on the dangers of pornography, conversation tips, and help for parents whose children may already be struggling with consumption.

When a Sheep Has Wandered

There is more to know about the dangers of pornography, but the shepherd's most crucial test comes when a sheep has wandered.

We will continue with this vital topic in **Chapter 13**, exploring practical and empathetic suggestions for parents whose child has fallen into this dark pit.

Inspiration from the Holy Scriptures

The commitment of the shepherd to his moral duty must be resolute and modeled for his children:

"I will not look with approval on anything that is vile. I hate what faithless people do; I will have no part in it." – Psalm 101:3 (NIV)

This verse expresses a commitment to choose to avoid anything morally wrong or harmful. As family shepherds, it is our responsibility to pass along that conviction, teaching our children to guard their hearts and minds from the vile content that seeks to prey on them.

Questions for Reflection and Discussion

The Predator is a Powerful Industry

- **The Scope of the Threat:** The global adult industry is estimated to be worth **over $60 billion** and targets children through various funnels (social media, gaming ads). How does knowing the **massive financial power and intentional marketing strategy** of this "predator" increase your sense of urgency regarding your protective role?

- **Accidental Exposure:** Research shows the average age of first exposure is around **12-13 years old**, often occurring unintentionally or via social media apps. What specific, proactive steps have you taken this month to address the dangers of **cross-platform advertising** and **unintentional exposure** on the devices used by your children?

- **The Father's Model (Psalm 101:3):** The commitment is to **"not look with approval on anything that is vile."** How well are you modeling this standard in your own life (media choices, online habits, and conversations), ensuring that your example does not create a hypocritical loophole for your children to walk through?

Grave Hazards to the Young Flock

- **Distorted Views and Normalization:** Pornography normalizes unhealthy behaviors, objectification, and distorted views of sexuality. As a father, what are the **key family values** regarding respect, consent, and healthy relationships that you need to articulate clearly and consistently to counteract these damaging narratives?

- **Emotional Distress:** Young minds struggle to differentiate fantasy from reality, leading to anxiety and inadequacy. How do you create an environment where your children feel safe enough to come to you immediately if they are confused, scared, or exposed to content that has caused them **emotional distress**?

- **Impact on Development:** Exposure can interfere with the child's ability to form stable, healthy relationships later in life. What is one way you can **intentionally invest** in teaching your child the building blocks of a healthy relationship (e.g., communication, empathy, conflict resolution) this week to safeguard their future relational capacity?

Navigating the Difficult Conversation

- **Start Early and Build Gradually:** Consistent, age-appropriate conversations are more effective than one "big talk." If your youngest child is a "lamb" (elementary age), what is the first, simple concept (body safety, appropriate touch) you can introduce **this week** to lay the groundwork for future discussions?

- **The Shepherd's Guidance:** The conversation should be framed around **honesty, accuracy, and core values**. If your child were to ask you tomorrow about something they accidentally saw online, what is the **first question** you would ask them to prioritize listening and non-judgmental understanding over immediate advice or anger?

- **Practical Protection:** The shepherd is responsible for the safety of the fold. Besides conversation, what **specific,**

technical safety measures (filters, monitoring software, device rules) do you currently have in place to fulfill your duty to monitor technology use appropriately and reduce the risk of harmful exposure for minors in your care?

CHAPTER 13
The Dark Valley (Part 2): Rescuing the Wandering Lamb

In the previous chapter, we established that the family shepherd must actively shield his flock from the hazard of pornography and engage in proactive, age-appropriate conversations. Now, we must address the situation when, despite a shepherd's best efforts, a young lamb has wandered into this dangerous territory.

This chapter focuses on the practical steps for **recognizing the signs of pornography use** and, most importantly, **how to respond with love, strength, and guidance** when you discover your child has been exposed.

Recognizing the Signs: A Shepherd's Vigilance

While the shepherd's heart hopes to prevent his child's exposure to porn, his eyes must be open to signs of distress. These signs can also indicate other issues, but they warrant the shepherd's attentive concern:

Behavioral Changes in the Young Lamb:

- **Increased Secrecy:** The child begins spending **more time alone**, especially in private spaces like bedrooms. They might suddenly clear their browsing history, increase incognito browsing, or **password-protect devices** without a clear reason.

- **Mood or Social Withdrawal:** Watch for irritability, mood swings, or signs of depression. They may exhibit **social withdrawal** or isolation from friends and family, or changes in sleep patterns and appetite.

- **Decline in Focus:** A noticeable **decline in academic performance**, missed assignments, or decreased focus in school.

- **Increased Sexualized Behavior or Language:** The child might begin using sexually explicit language, drawing sexual images, or showing an **unusual or advanced knowledge** of sexual topics that is inappropriate for their age.

Potential Indicators of Problematic Use:

These signs suggest the behavior is becoming more compulsive or harmful:

- **Compulsive Behavior:** Difficulty controlling or limiting porn use, spending excessive amounts of time viewing it, or continuing to use it despite **negative consequences** (e.g., missed sleep, poor grades).

- **Escalating Consumption:** Seeking out increasingly extreme or graphic content to maintain the same level of stimulus.

- **Impact on Relationships:** Difficulty forming or maintaining healthy relationships, or noticeable negative changes in their attitudes towards intimacy and respect.

Important Consideration: It's crucial to avoid making assumptions based on a single sign. If you are concerned, do not act alone; seek guidance from your parenting partner, a trusted adult, or a professional counselor.

My Child Has Discovered Porn. Now What?

Discovering that your child is viewing pornography is a challenging moment, one that tests the shepherd's resolve and compassion. Your response in the immediate aftermath will have a profound impact on your child's willingness to seek help.

The Shepherd's Six-Step Rescue Plan:

1. Stay Calm and Approach with Understanding:

- **Resist the urge to panic or react angrily.** A calm and measured response is crucial to maintaining the path of effective communication.

- **Avoid shaming or blaming.** This will shut down communication immediately and push the child deeper into secrecy.

- Remember that **curiosity about sexuality is normal**, especially during adolescence. Your focus must be on **guiding their curiosity**, not condemning their person.

2. Initiate a Calm and Open Conversation:

- Choose a **private and comfortable setting**. Begin by expressing your unconditional love and concern for your child, rather than your disappointment.

o **Listen more than you talk.** Your goal is to understand their perspective and motivations.

o Ask **open-ended questions** in a non-accusatory tone: "What have you been watching?" "How does it make you feel?" "Do you have any questions about what you have seen?" (Be prepared to have **multiple conversations**; this is an ongoing process.)

3. Provide Education and Guidance:

o Discuss the **unrealistic and often harmful portrayals** of relationships, sexuality, and bodies in pornography.

o Explain the potential negative impacts, such as distorted views of intimacy and the potential for addiction.

o Offer **accurate information** about healthy sexuality, respect, and **consent** — emphasizing that true intimacy is based on mutual care, not exploitation.

o Discuss **online safety** explicitly: the dangers of online predators and the **permanence of online content**.

4. Set Boundaries and Implement Safeguards:

- Establish **clear, firm rules and expectations** regarding internet and device usage.

- Use **parental control software** or filtering apps to filter content and monitor online activity.

- **Keep computers and devices in common areas** of the house to remove the temptation of secretive use.

- Have **open conversations** about *why* these boundaries are in place (emphasizing it is for their protection, not punishment).

5. Seek Professional Help if Needed:

- If you are deeply concerned about the compulsive nature of the use, or if your child is struggling emotionally, **seek guidance from a qualified therapist or counselor**. A professional can provide support and strategies for both you and your child.

6. Ongoing Support and Communication:

- This is not a one-time event; it is a long-term commitment. **Be patient and understanding;** changes in behavior take time.

- Maintain an open, honest channel of communication, ensuring they feel safe enough to ask questions and express concerns in the future.

More Helpful Resources for the Shepherd

- **Professional Counseling:** Therapists and counselors specializing in youth or family issues can provide targeted support.

- **Focus on the Family:** This organization offers resources, articles, and advice for families dealing with problematic pornography use, including specific guidance on how to respond to a child's suspected use.

- **The National Sexual Violence Resource Center (NSVRC):** Provides information and support related to preventing sexual exploitation.

Inspiration from the Holy Scriptures

The most excellent safeguard for the flock is the purity of the shepherd's own heart. As fathers, we must model excellent behaviors, which, of course, include abstaining from pornography and other spiritually unhealthy things.

*"Above all else, **guard your heart**, for everything you do flows from it." — Proverbs 4:23 (NIV)*

By actively **guarding our own hearts** from unwholesome content, we set a clear, righteous example. What is in our hearts will eventually come out. Therefore, the shepherd does well to fill his heart and mind with the **Word of God** instead (Psalm 119:11), ensuring that his guidance of the flock flows from a place of purity and truth

Questions for Reflection and Discussion

Recognizing the Signs: A Shepherd's Vigilance

- **Increased Secrecy and Withdrawal:** The shepherd's vigilance requires him to notice subtle shifts in behavior. Which of the listed signs (e.g., increased secrecy, clearing browsing history, social withdrawal) would be the **most difficult** for you to notice in your child's current routine, and what intentional steps can you take to increase your awareness?

- **Problematic Use:** Signs of **compulsive behavior** or **escalating consumption** suggest the need for professional intervention. If you observed a child continuing this behavior despite negative consequences (poor grades, missed sleep), how quickly would you be willing to set aside shame and **seek guidance from a qualified therapist**?

- **Guard Your Heart (Proverbs 4:23):** The chapter stresses that the most excellent safeguard is the **purity of the shepherd's own heart**. What personal, protective discipline (meditating on Scripture, monitoring your own media use, accountability) are you implementing to ensure that the guidance you give your child flows from a place of purity and truth?

The Shepherd's Six-Step Rescue Plan

- **Step 1: Staying Calm and Resisting Shame:** The most critical step is to **resist the urge to panic or react angrily**. Reflect on the last time you were deeply disappointed or frustrated by your child's behavior. What mental or spiritual pause mechanism do you need to implement to ensure your first response is motivated by **love and concern**, rather than shaming and blame?

- **Step 2: Listening More Than Talking:** The goal is to **understand their perspective and motivations** by asking non-accusatory, open-ended questions. If you had to choose only one, what is the most important thing you would want to **understand** about your child's exposure — the content they saw, or how it made them feel? Why?

- **Step 3: Providing Accurate Guidance:** The focus is on offering accurate information about **healthy sexuality, respect, and consent**, contrasting it with exploitative content. If your child is viewing pornography, how can you most effectively frame the discussion around **God's design for intimacy** as mutual care and respect, rather than focusing solely on prohibition?

Implementation and Ongoing Support

- **Step 4: Boundaries and Safeguards:** The shepherd must implement clear, firm rules and safeguards (e.g., parental control software, devices in common areas). Which is harder for you: **setting the initial firm boundary** or **maintaining the consistency** of that boundary over the long term? What is your strategy for ensuring consistency?

- **Step 6: Long-Term Commitment:** Rescuing a wandering lamb is a **long-term commitment** requiring patience and ongoing support. Beyond the initial conversation, what is one concrete way you can commit to **maintaining an open, honest channel of communication** over the next six months to ensure your child feels safe asking future questions?

- **The Shepherd's Authority:** The effectiveness of the rescue plan hinges on the child's willingness to trust their shepherd. In what specific, recent action have you demonstrated to your child that you are a **trusted, non-judgmental guide** they can safely turn to in times of shame or confusion?

CHAPTER 14
The Dark Valley (Part 3) Guarding the Flock from Abuse and Neglect

The shepherd's duty is to keep his flock not only nourished and guided but fundamentally **safe** from predators and harm. Tragically, in the 21st century, the gravest harm often comes from within the community, sometimes even within the home. **Child abuse and neglect** are severe threats that the father-shepherd must understand and actively combat. Every child deserves to live happily, healthily, and securely, and it is our solemn privilege to ensure this reality for our own and our neighbors' children.

The Prevalence of Child Maltreatment

Gathering precise figures on child abuse is challenging because many cases go tragically **unreported** due to fear, shame, and lack of awareness. However, available data provide a sobering picture:

- **1 in 7 children** in the U.S. has experienced child abuse or neglect in the past year, according to sources like the Centers for Disease Control and Prevention (CDC). This is almost certainly an underestimate.[ix]

- **Neglect** is the most common form of child maltreatment.

- **Young children** are the most vulnerable, with the highest rates of victimization occurring in **infants and toddlers**.

- Child abuse affects children of all backgrounds. However, children from **BIPOC (Black, Indigenous, and People of Color) communities** have a **higher rate of victimization** compared to the general population.

Prevention and intervention efforts are not just helpful; they are **crucial** to protecting the next generation.

The Family Shepherd's Strategy for Prevention

Prevention is a critical, proactive responsibility. The shepherd must be well-informed and equipped with the knowledge to safeguard his fold.

1. Understanding Child Abuse (Knowing the Danger)

- **Types of Abuse:** You must be able to name the predators:

    - **Physical abuse:** Inflicting or attempting physical harm.

    - **Sexual abuse:** Any sexual activity with a child.

    - **Emotional abuse:** Inflicting psychological harm through words or actions.

    - **Neglect:** Failing to provide basic needs like food, shelter, medical care, or supervision.

- **Recognizing Signs:** Be aware of physical, behavioral, and emotional indicators. **Unexplained injuries, sudden changes in behavior, poor hygiene, or a profound fear of certain adults** can be warning signs.

2. Creating a Safe Environment (Securing the Fold)

- **Nurturing Relationships:** Foster **strong, positive relationships** with your children. **Open communication** is crucial for building trust. Validate their feelings and provide consistent emotional support.

- **Setting Boundaries:** Establish **clear and consistent rules**. Teach children about the difference between **appropriate and inappropriate touching**. Empower them to say **"no"** to anything that makes them uncomfortable and assure them they will be **believed and supported**.

- **Supervision and Monitoring:** Be aware of who your children are interacting with, both online and offline. Monitor their internet and social media activity and **know who is supervising your children** when they are outside of your care.

3. Building Protective Factors (Strengthening the Sheep)

- **Parenting Skills:** Learn and practice **positive parenting techniques**. Model healthy ways to manage stress and anger. Remember to seek support when your burdens feel heavy.

- **Community Support:** Build a reliable support network of family, friends, and community resources. A strong community is a safer environment.

- **Education:** Educate your children about **personal safety** and healthy relationships. Teach them to identify **trusted adults** (beyond their parents) they can talk to.

4. Taking Action (Intervening to Protect)

- **Reporting Suspected Abuse:** If you suspect child abuse or neglect, you may have a moral, and in many jurisdictions, a legal duty to **report it to the appropriate authorities**. Contact your local child protective services or law enforcement immediately. **Reporting can save a child's life.**

- **Preventing Abuse in Your Community:** Support local child abuse prevention programs, volunteer your time, and be a **responsible, caring member of your community**.

What Fathers Can Do Together: Amplifying the Impact

Fathers working together can create a powerful force for positive change, fortifying the community shield against child abuse and neglect.

Building Supportive Networks:

- o **Fatherhood Groups:** Create or join groups that provide a safe space for sharing experiences and solutions. Platforms like the Fathering Strong®ˣ mobile app can organize virtual groups for peer support and mentorship.

- o **Mentoring:** Older or more experienced fathers can mentor younger fathers, guiding those facing challenges or lacking positive role models.

Promoting Positive Parenting:

- o **Education and Training:** Organize workshops on positive parenting skills, anger management, and effective discipline.

- o **Modeling Healthy Behavior:** Fathers must collectively model healthy relationships, respectful communication, and appropriate emotional expression. This includes unequivocally demonstrating **respect for women and children.**

Raising Awareness and Taking Action:

- o **Public Awareness Campaigns:** Collaborate on campaigns to educate the community about prevention.

- o **Supporting Victims and Families:** Work together to support victims of abuse by providing emotional support, practical assistance, and access to resources.

- o **Challenging Harmful Norms:** Work to challenge societal norms that promote violence or condone abusive behavior. **Promote healthy masculinity** that aligns with the servant-leader model.

Inspiration from the Holy Scriptures

Our greatest inspiration comes from the Ultimate Protector. The Father God models for us what it is to be a refuge, and defender for those under His care:

"He who dwells in the shelter of the Most High shall abide under the shadow of the Almighty. I will say of the Lord, 'He is my refuge and my fortress, my God in whom I trust.'" — Psalm 91:1-2 (MEV)

Our responsibility and privilege are to emulate this protection, doing all we can to make sure that all the children within our reach are happy, healthy, and safe from abuse and neglect.

Questions for Reflection and Discussion

The Reality of Maltreatment and Prevention

- **Prevalence and Vulnerability:** The chapter states that approximately **1 in 7 children** experience abuse or neglect, with **neglect** being the most common form. How does this sobering data challenge you to increase your vigilance against the **passive threat of neglect** (failing to provide basic emotional, medical, or supervisory needs) in your own home?

- **Recognizing Signs:** The shepherd must recognize the signs of danger (physical, behavioral, emotional). What is your current system for monitoring your child's well-being? Name one **specific behavioral change** (e.g., sudden secrecy, mood swings, fear of an adult) that would immediately prompt you to stop what you are doing and investigate with calm, focused attention?

- **Setting Boundaries and Empowering:** A key prevention strategy is **setting boundaries** and **empowering children to say "no."** What is the clearest, most consistent message you communicate to your children about **appropriate touch** and their **right to safety**, ensuring they know they will be believed and supported when they speak up?

The Family Shepherd's Strategy

- **Nurturing Relationships (Trust): Open communication** and **trust** are critical for the child to report harm. How can you model and practice **positive parenting techniques** this week to validate your child's feelings and foster the strong, positive relationship required for them to trust you in a crisis?

- **Supervision and Monitoring:** Supervision extends to knowing who is interacting with your children **online and offline.** Beyond knowing their friends, who is supervising your child when they are outside of your care (babysitters, coaches, teachers), and what systems do you have in place to **vet and monitor** these individuals?

- **Taking Action (Reporting):** If you suspect child abuse or neglect (in your home or a neighbor's), you may have a legal duty to report it. If you were faced with suspicion, what is the **immediate, non-negotiable step** you would take to contact appropriate authorities (Child Protective Services or law enforcement)? Why is **action** more important than fear or embarrassment in this situation?

Fathers Working Together: Amplifying the Impact

- **Building Supportive Networks:** The chapter advocates for fathers joining or creating groups (like Fathering Strong) for **peer support and mentorship.** What is the biggest challenge in your fathering right now, and who is the **trusted, more experienced**

father in your community you could reach out to for advice and support?

- **Modeling Healthy Masculinity:** Fathers must collectively model **healthy masculinity** that aligns with the servant-leader model. What is one way you can commit to **unequivocally demonstrating respect for women and children** in your public and private life this week, thereby challenging the harmful norms that condone abusive behavior?

- **The Ultimate Protector (Psalm 91:1-2):** God is our **refuge and fortress**. How does the knowledge that God is the Ultimate Protector and Defender inspire and strengthen you in your commitment to be a **refuge** for your own children and a defender for the vulnerable children in your community?

CHAPTER 15
The Dark Valley (Part 4): Supporting a Lamb at Risk of Self-Harm

The father-shepherd's duties include traversing the most dangerous terrain. Today, one of the most heartbreaking and complex hazards facing our young flock is the risk of **self-harm**, also known as non-suicidal self-injury (NSSI). Research indicates this is more prevalent than many realize, often serving as a desperate coping mechanism for deep emotional distress. Protecting children from this hazard requires a multifaceted approach focused on **open communication, emotional support, and professional intervention**.

Understanding the Wounded Lamb

Self-harm is often a sign of **underlying emotional distress**. Dr. Melissa Butler, a clinical psychologist, notes that in young children, it's often due to an inability to express feelings or have their needs met. In adolescents, it may stem from feelings of hopelessness or a sense of worthlessness.

Prevalence and Risk Factors:
- **Prevalence:** NSSI occurs in children and adolescents, with rates generally higher in adolescents. It is increasingly common, even among children younger than 11.[xi]

- **Mental Health Conditions:** Children with depression, anxiety, or trauma are at **increased risk**.

- **Neurodevelopmental Disorders:** Self-injurious behavior (SIB) is a concerning and prevalent issue among children with **autism spectrum disorder (ASD)** and other neurodevelopmental disorders (NDDs).[xii]

- **Social Factors:** Bullying, social isolation, and exposure to online self-harm communities also contribute to the risk.

The shepherd must note that **suicidal ideation and self-harm are becoming more common in younger children**. Early intervention and support are essential.

Strategies for Supporting Your Child

The shepherd's response must prioritize connection and help the child develop healthy coping mechanisms.

1. Foster Open Communication (The Open Gate):

- **Create a Safe Space:** Let your child know they can talk to you about **anything without judgment**. Actively listen and **validate their feelings**, even if you don't understand them.

- **Regular Check-ins:** Have **consistent conversations** about their emotional well-being. Pay close attention to changes in their mood or behavior.

- **Educate About Emotions:** Help them identify and express their feelings in healthy ways. Teach them healthy coping mechanisms for managing difficult emotions.

2. Recognize Warning Signs (The Shepherd's Watch):

The shepherd must be vigilant and aware of subtle shifts in the fold:

- **Changes in Behavior:** Withdrawal from social activities, increased irritability or anger, changes in eating or sleeping patterns, or a decline in academic performance.

- **Physical Signs:** Unexplained cuts, bruises, or burns. **Wearing long sleeves or pants even in warm weather** to hide injuries. Isolation in their room for extended periods.

- **Emotional Signs:** Expressions of **hopelessness, worthlessness, or helplessness**; increased anxiety or panic attacks, and preoccupation with death or dying.

3. Create a Safe Environment (Securing the Fold):

- **Limit Access to Harmful Items: Secure sharp objects, medications, and any other potentially dangerous items.** Be mindful of any items that could be used for self-harm.

- **Monitor Online Activity:** Be aware of your child's social media and online use. Educate them about the risks of harmful **online self-harm communities**.

- **Promote Healthy Coping Mechanisms:** Encourage physical activity, creative expression, and relaxation techniques. Help them develop a support system of trusted friends and family.

4. Seek Professional Help (Calling for Aid):

- **Mental Health Professionals:** If you suspect your child is self-harming, **seek professional help immediately.** Therapists can provide guidance and support for both the child and the family.

- **Crisis Hotlines: Take all threats of self-harm seriously.** Know the critical resources:

  o **National Suicide & Crisis Lifeline: 988**

  o **Crisis Text Line: Text HOME to 741741**

Key Considerations: Early intervention is crucial. Self-harm is often a symptom, and it is important to address the underlying emotional issues. Be patient and supportive; recovery takes time.

What Fathers Can Do Together: Mutual Support

Fathers of children at risk face unique, intense challenges. **Peer support** can be incredibly valuable for maintaining the shepherd's strength.

Create Safe Spaces for Sharing:

  o **Establish Support Groups:** These can be online or in-person, providing a **confidential, judgment-free space** for fathers to share experiences and feelings.

  o **Informal Gatherings:** Casual meetups can offer a vital sense of community and understanding.

Offer Practical Support and Advice:

- Share Coping Strategies: Fathers can share what has worked for them in communicating with their children, such as active listening techniques, and managing their own stress.

- Offer Respite: Sometimes, the greatest help is simply offering to **watch another father's children for a few hours** to provide much-needed relief and a chance for self-care.

Provide Emotional Validation and Understanding:

- Acknowledge the Challenges: Validate their feelings of fear, frustration, and helplessness. Let them know they are **not alone**.

- Combat Stigma: Support each other in challenging negative stereotypes and promoting **open conversations about mental health** — especially important for fathers who often feel pressure to be stoic.

Focus on Self-Care:

- Encourage Self-Care Practices: Remind each other of the importance of taking care of their own mental and physical health.

- Promote Healthy Coping: Help each other identify and avoid unhealthy coping mechanisms (e.g., substance abuse or isolation).

Inspiration from the Holy Scriptures

The shepherd's strength to care for the wounded lamb comes from the support of his fellow laborers:

"So encourage each other and build each other up, just as you are already doing." - 1 Thessalonians 5:11 (NLT)

Fathers are **better together**. Seek or create opportunities to encourage another father. In doing so, you may find the support and strength you need for yourself to continue guiding your flock through the valleys.

Questions for Reflection and Discussion

Understanding the Wounded Lamb

- **Self-Harm as a Coping Mechanism:** Self-harm is often a desperate way for a child to cope with intense **emotional distress** (hopelessness, worthlessness). If you notice unexplained cuts, burns, or the wearing of long sleeves in warm weather, what is the most important thing you need to communicate to your child **immediately** to create a safe space for them to open up?

- **The Prevalence and Risk:** Research shows that self-harm is becoming more common, even in younger children, often linked to mental health conditions, neurodevelopmental disorders, or social factors like **bullying and online exposure.**

  - What active steps are you taking to monitor and intervene against **bullying or social isolation** in your child's life?

  - If you have a child with a neurodevelopmental disorder (like ASD), what **specific communication strategies** do you use to help them express their feelings healthily?

Strategies for Supporting Your Child

- **Foster Open Communication (The Open Gate):** To create a non-judgmental safe space, you must first **validate your child's feelings**, even if you don't understand them. When your child expresses sadness or anger, do you tend to respond by trying to **solve the problem** or by simply **listening and validating** their emotion ("That sounds incredibly hard")? Which is more helpful right now?

- **Recognize Warning Signs (The Shepherd's Watch):** Sudden **changes in behavior** (withdrawal, irritability, changes in sleep/appetite) are key indicators. What is one way you can institute **regular check-ins** with your child (e.g., dedicated 15 minutes at bedtime, a weekly one-on-one activity) to pay closer attention to these subtle shifts?

- **Create a Safe Environment:** You must **limit access to harmful items** and **monitor online activity**. Beyond putting away sharp objects, how are you promoting and encouraging healthy coping mechanisms (e.g., physical activity, creative expression) in your family's routine to replace self-destructive behaviors?

Professional Help and Mutual Support

- **Seeking Professional Help (Calling for Aid):** If you suspect self-harm, the chapter advises seeking **professional help immediately**. What is the number for your **National Suicide & Crisis Lifeline** (988 in the US), and where is this number displayed in your home for quick access?

- **The Shepherd's Self-Care:** Fathers of children at risk face intense stress. The support of fellow fathers can be critical for maintaining your strength. What specific **self-care practice** (physical, mental, or spiritual) will you commit to this week, and which trusted father will you ask to hold you accountable to it?

- **Encourage and Build Up (1 Thessalonians 5:11): Mutual support** among fathers combats stigma and prevents isolation. Is there another father in your circle who is currently going through a difficult valley? What is one way you can actively **encourage and build up** him this week, thereby strengthening the community fold?

CHAPTER 16
The Dark Valley (Part 5): Youth Gambling—A Shepherd's Guide to the New Normal

The "game" your teen is playing may not be a game at all: **it might be gambling**. This is a startling reality for today's shepherds, especially considering that problem gambling rates are significantly **higher among teens than adults**. As the loving father and protector, you must be informed and equipped to address this rapidly growing trend.

The New Trends in Gambling: Not Your Grandfather's Poker Game

Gambling is no longer confined to casinos or back rooms; it is now on your children's **phones, consoles, and advertised everywhere**. You cannot watch a major sporting event on television without being bombarded with betting ads, which normalize the connection between sports and wagering.

Emerging Gambling Trends: A Shepherd's Concern

Online Sports Betting & Media Exposure

- **Concern:** Major sports events are saturated with betting ads, normalizing the connection. Teens can easily create online accounts by lying about their age.

"Loot Boxes" in Video Games

- **Concern:** 31% of 11 to 16-year-olds have opened these chance-based items. Spending on loot boxes is directly linked to problem gambling severity.

"Skins" Gambling

- **Concern:** Betting with in-game items ('skins') on unregulated websites. 3% of 11 to 16-year-olds claim to have done this.

Prevalence

- **Concern:** 60 to 80% of high school students have gambled in the past year. Youth problem gambling rates (4 to 8%) are significantly higher than adult rates ($\sim$1%).

The Dangers: Why This Matters More Than Money

The teenage brain is still developing, making the young flock uniquely vulnerable. The risks associated with youth gambling are severe and extend far beyond financial loss.

- **The Underdeveloped Brain:** The **decision-making part** of the brain (prefrontal cortex) is not fully developed until the mid-20s, making teens more **impulsive** and less able to weigh risks and consequences.

- **Addiction and Mental Health:** Problem gambling is severely linked to **depression and anxiety, substance use problems** (teens who gamble are more likely to use drugs/alcohol), and tragically, **suicide** - gambling addiction has one of the highest suicide rates among all addictions.

- **Cascading Consequences:** Financial loss often leads to further destructive behaviors, including **lying, stealing, poor school performance, and strained family relationships.**

- **Early Onset:** Children introduced to "harmless betting" by age 12 are **four times more likely** to engage in problem gambling later.

Your Role: A Call to Action for the Family Shepherd

Research highlights the specific and critical influence of the **father's role** in either encouraging or preventing this hazard.

Your Unique Influence: Key Findings for Fathers

Role Modeling

- **Key Finding:** Parental gambling is a strong predictor of adolescent gambling participation and problems. If the shepherd gambles, the lamb is more likely to follow.

Co-Gambling

- **Key Finding:** Fathers report a higher rate of **co-gambling** (gambling alongside) with their adolescents than mothers.

Awareness & Concern

- **Key Finding:** Fathers report higher rates of **awareness** of adolescent gambling and simulated gambling than mothers, but they also report being **more concerned**

If you suspect this enemy is near your flock, or see it, **take immediate action!**

Protective Strategies for the Family Shepherd

Here are the practical, actionable steps to shield your children from this pervasive danger.

1. Talk and Educate (The Shepherd's Voice):

- **Don't Wait:** Start conversations about gambling risks **as early as six years old** and continue the conversation as they grow.

- **Explain the Odds:** Explain that **gambling is a business set up to take money** and that "the house always wins." Use relatable comparisons for odds to highlight the impossibility of winning.

- **Talk About Gaming:** Discuss in-game purchases like **loot boxes** and "skins," and help them understand how these mechanics are designed to mimic the **thrill of betting,** thereby normalizing gambling behavior.

- **Make it a Discussion:** Children whose parents talk to them about the risks of gambling are **less likely to develop a problem**. Ask your child what they think. The goal is open dialogue and trust.

2. Set Boundaries and Model Behavior (The Shepherd's Example):

- **Model Healthy Behavior: Don't gamble!** If you do, be highly conscious of your own moderate gambling (e.g., lottery tickets) and **unequivocally avoid co-gambling with your child**. Do not use monetary rewards for family wagers.

- **Establish Tech Rules:** Set clear limits for screen time and gaming. **Remove devices from bedrooms** and limit access to online gambling sites.

- **Financial Control: Limit your youth's access to your credit cards** for in-game or online purchases, requiring an explanation before any purchase.

3. Recognize the Warning Signs (The Shepherd's Vigilance):

- A sudden, intense interest in sports scores or stats.

- Unexplained mood swings, anxiety, or depression.

- **Missing money** or frequently asking to borrow money.

- Decline in grades or less interest in usual hobbies.

- Increased time online, especially being **secretive** about it.

Inspiration from the Holy Scriptures

The wise father must model a strong work ethic, which gambling directly undermines. The Bible instructs us to supply our own needs and those of our families by engaging in **productive labor** (2 Thessalonians 3:10; 1 Timothy 5:8).

*"Wealth from **gambling quickly disappears**; wealth from **hard work** grows."* — *Proverbs 13:11 (The Living Bible)*

Gambling undercuts the work ethic that has been part of God's design since the beginning. The wise father will model hard work and will avoid setting a bad example by gambling away his money, thus protecting his children from both financial and spiritual risk. Take the lead in preventative measures; have a conversation with your youth tonight.

Resources

Prevention starts at home with open communication and impeccable modeling. If you or your child needs help, the most widely recognized and confidential national resource for problem gambling in the United States is:

National Problem Gambling Helpline

- **Contact:**

    o   Call: **1-800-522-4700**

    o   Text: **800GAM (4262)**

    o   Website: **ncpgambling.org**

This chapter effectively introduces the modern "dark valley" of **youth gambling**, highlighting new trends (online betting, loot boxes, skins), the unique vulnerability of the teenage brain, and the crucial preventative role of the father.

Here are "Questions for Reflection and Discussion" drafted for Chapter 16, tailored to men and fathers:

Questions for Reflection and Discussion

The New Normal: Identifying the Danger

- **Normalizing the Risk:** Major sports events are saturated with betting ads, normalizing gambling. What is your family's strategy for addressing the constant exposure to betting ads in media (e.g., watching sports, social media)? Do you simply ignore them, or do you actively **use them as teaching moments** to explain the danger?

- **Loot Boxes and Skins Gambling:** Up to 80% of high school students have gambled in the past year, and "loot boxes" are directly linked to problem gambling severity. How often do you discuss in-game purchases and rewards with your children, and what are you doing to help them understand that these mechanics are designed to **mimic the thrill of betting**?

- **The Underdeveloped Brain:** The teenage brain's **prefrontal cortex** (decision-making) is still developing, making teens highly impulsive and less able to weigh risks. Given this vulnerability, what specific financial boundaries or tech rules are you implementing to safeguard your impulsive teen from **online gambling or easy in-game spending**?

Your Unique Influence: A Call to Action

- **Role Modeling: Parental gambling** is a strong predictor of adolescent gambling problems. Reflect on your own relationship with chance and wealth (lottery tickets, fantasy leagues, stock market risks). What is one way you can immediately model a healthier, more consistent financial work ethic that aligns with the instruction in **Proverbs 13:11** ("Wealth from hard work grows")?

- **Co-Gambling:** Fathers report a higher rate of **co-gambling** with adolescents than mothers. Have you ever placed a harmless wager or bought a lottery ticket *with* your child? Why must the family shepherd **unequivocally avoid** all forms of co-gambling to protect their flock?

- **Early Onset:** Children introduced to betting by age 12 are **four times more likely** to engage in problem gambling later. If you have younger children (under 12), what is the non-negotiable step you will take this week to **start the conversation** about gambling risks and the truth about odds?

Protective Strategies and Vigilance

- **Financial Control:** The shepherd must maintain financial control to protect the sheep. Beyond limiting credit card access, what system do you use to ensure your youth's **in-game or online purchases** require accountability and an explanation before they happen?

- **Warning Signs: Unexplained mood swings, missing money, a decline in grades, or secretive online time** are key warning signs. If you noticed a sudden, intense interest in sports scores or stats, how would you initiate a **calm, open, non-accusatory dialogue** to investigate the cause of the interest?

- **Resources and Support:** Gambling addiction has one of the **highest suicide rates** among all addictions. If you or your child needs help, you can call or text the National Problem Gambling Helpline at **1-800-522-4700**. Why is knowing this resource and being willing to **seek immediate, confidential aid** the ultimate act of protective shepherding?

CHAPTER 17
The Dark Valley (Part 6): Guiding Through Entertainment Hazards

The responsible shepherd must **protect his flock** from all the dangers in the surrounding landscape. Today, one of the most pervasive yet often overlooked hazards to your family's spiritual and emotional well-being is the vast, frequently toxic landscape of **entertainment choices**. As fathers, we hold the primary responsibility, alongside our parenting partner, to screen and select the content that enters our fold. Obviously, **we must be present and engaged in guiding** those choices.

This chapter provides **five key considerations** to help you navigate the entertainment wilderness and select wholesome, strengthening options for your family.

Key #1: Align with the Shepherd's Values

Before consuming any form of entertainment, the shepherd must first consult his **moral compass**. What are the non-negotiable values and beliefs that govern your household? Look for content that **aligns with your family's moral compass** and actively avoids promoting destructive, harmful, or negative behaviors.

For example, if the shepherd values **nonviolence** and peace within the fold, this means actively avoiding movies, shows, games, and books that feature gratuitous bloodshed, fighting, mayhem, and killing.

The Shepherd's Warning: The Possible Impacts of Violent Media

The shepherd must be aware of the wolves that seek to enter the gate. Exposure to violent or morally compromising media can have subtle yet lasting effects on the young minds in your care:

- **Increased Aggression:** Studies have consistently found a link between exposure to violent media and increased aggressive behavior in children.

- **Desensitization to Harm:** Repeated exposure to violence can lead to **desensitization**, meaning children become less emotionally affected by the portrayal of suffering, which can decrease their **empathy** for real-life victims.

- **Normalization of the Unacceptable:** When violence is constantly present or even rewarded in entertainment, it contributes to the **normalization** of unacceptable behaviors, making them seem **inevitable or acceptable**.

The dedicated shepherd is not an ostrich, burying his head in the sand. He understands that while the media is one of many factors in development, he must actively guard the gate and select content that promotes the values of kindness, patience, and love.

Key #2: Consider Age-Appropriateness

Just as a shepherd knows that a young lamb cannot handle the same terrain as a mature sheep, you must ensure that entertainment content is **suitable for your children's ages and maturity levels**. Rely on the tools available to you.

The shepherd must **pay attention to ratings and content advisories**, which are essentially warning signs placed along the entertainment path:

Understanding Entertainment Rating Systems

Movies

- **Rating System Example:** MPAA: G, PG, **PG-13**, **R**, NC-17

- **Shepherd's Note:** **PG-13** means Parents Strongly Cautioned (may be unsuitable for children under 13). **R** means Restricted.

Television

- **Rating System Example:** TV Parental Guidelines: TV-Y, TV-PG, **TV-14**, **TV-MA**

- **Shepherd's Note:** **TV-MA** means Mature Audiences (content is not suitable for children). **TV-14** is suitable for children 14 and older.

Video Games

- **Rating System Example:** ESRB: EC (Early Childhood), E (Everyone), **T (Teen), M (Mature)**

- **Shepherd's Note: T** is for Teen (13+). **M** is for Mature (17+). Do not rationalize exposing your young children to M-rated content.

In addition to ratings, always look for **Content Advisories** that provide specific information on sensitive material like **Violence, Language, Sexual Content, or Drug/Alcohol Use.** Understanding these systems is a vital part of making **informed decisions** about what your children are exposed to.

Key #3: Seek Positive Themes

The best entertainment options are not merely *harmless*; they are **uplifting and inspiring.** The wise shepherd seeks out stories that are like good spring grass — nourishing and life-giving.

Look for content that reinforces **positive themes** such as kindness, compassion, honesty, responsibility, and perseverance. These narratives can inspire your family and provide real-world examples of virtuous living.

Examples of Nourishing Content:

- **Movies:** *The Lion King* (courage, responsibility), *Toy Story* (friendship, adventure), *Up* (love, fulfilling dreams), *Coco* (family, heritage).

- **TV Shows:** *Bluey* (play, imagination, family bonds), *Daniel Tiger's Neighborhood* (emotional intelligence, problem-solving), *The Good Place* (philosophical comedy about ethics and becoming a better person).

- **Books:** Explore the local library and find wholesome books to read together. Shared reading time is a fantastic opportunity to model the love of learning.

You may also be interested in films and shows that feature **faith-based or Christian themes** that directly reinforce your family's spiritual foundation.

Key #4: Encourage Critical Thinking

Select entertainment that warrants deeper consideration and sparks meaningful **discussions**. The shepherd doesn't want sheep who blindly follow the leader; he wants his children to be **wise and discerning**.

Encourage your children to analyze characters, plotlines, and underlying messages:

- **Ask penetrating questions:** "What choice did that character make, and what were the consequences?"

- **Discuss the message:** "What was the main idea of that story? Do you agree with it?"

- **Analyze motives:** "Why do you think that person behaved that way?"

This process helps them develop **critical thinking skills** and form their own well-reasoned opinions, protecting them from simply absorbing whatever message the media presents.

Key #5: Prioritize Quality Over Popularity

In the realm of entertainment, do not be swayed by **hype or popularity**. A crowd may rush toward a shallow, low-quality source of water, but the wise shepherd seeks out a deep, clean well.

Focus on quality content that is well-made, engaging, and **meaningful**. Look for reviews from trusted sources that align with your family's values. By following this guideline, you create a family entertainment experience that is both enjoyable and enriching, ensuring that every moment spent consuming media is a value-added experience for the fold.

Inspiration from the Holy Scriptures

The wisdom of the father-shepherd is demonstrated by the enduring quality of the home he builds and the spiritual wealth within it:

*"A house is built by **wisdom**. It is made strong by understanding, and by much learning, the rooms are filled with all **riches that are pleasing and of great worth**."* — *Proverbs* 24:3-4

Guiding your family's entertainment choices with wisdom and understanding ensures that your home is not filled with cultural junk food, but with "riches that are pleasing and of great worth."

Questions for Reflection and Discussion

Guiding Through Entertainment Hazards

- **The Primary Responsibility:** The shepherd holds the primary responsibility to **screen and select** the content that enters the fold. When was the last time you, as the father, took the initiative to **actively research and select** a movie, show, or game for the family based on its moral alignment, rather than simply letting your children choose based on popularity?

- **The Shepherd's Warning (Violent Media):** Exposure to violent media is linked to **increased aggression** and **desensitization to harm**. If a show or game is rated PG-13 (Parents Strongly Cautioned) for violence, what specific negative behavior or emotional response in your child would cause you to guard the gate and prohibit that content immediately?

- **Normalization of the Unacceptable:** When morally compromising behaviors are constantly present or even rewarded in the media, they become normalized. What is one **unacceptable behavior** (e.g., disrespect, cheating, gratuitous violence) that you frequently see normalized in popular media, and how are you actively **teaching your children to reject** that normalization?

Five Keys to Wholesome Choices

- **Key #1: Align with the Shepherd's Values:** What are the top three **non-negotiable values** (e.g., nonviolence, respect, humility) that govern your household? What are you doing this week to actively find content that **aligns** with these values, and what content are you actively **avoiding** because it promotes the opposite?

- **Key #2: Consider Age-Appropriateness:** The shepherd must pay attention to ratings (MPAA, TV Parental Guidelines, ESRB). Do you have a **firm, non-negotiable rule** regarding M-rated (Mature/17+) video games and R-rated (Restricted) movies? If you rationalize exposing younger children to restricted content, what specific evidence suggests that their **maturity level** can process that content healthily?

- **Key #3: Seek Positive Themes:** The best entertainment is **uplifting and inspiring.** Name one movie, show, or book your family has consumed in the last month that genuinely reinforced a positive theme like **kindness, compassion, or perseverance.** How can you increase the frequency of this "nourishing content"?

- **Key #4: Encourage Critical Thinking:** The shepherd wants **wise and discerning sheep**, not blind followers. What is one **penetrating question** you can ask your child tonight about the choices or motives of a character in a story, regardless of whether the content was "wholesome" or "concerning"?

- **Key #5: Prioritize Quality Over Popularity:** Focus on content that is **well-made, engaging, and meaningful**, not just popular. How do you find **trusted sources** for reviews and recommendations that align with your family's values, rather than relying solely on the consensus of the media market?

Building a House of Wisdom

- **Riches of Great Worth (Proverbs 24:3-4):** Guiding your choices ensures your home is filled with **"riches that are pleasing and of great worth,"** not cultural junk food. What is the one area of entertainment (TV, gaming, music) in your home where you need to apply **wisdom and understanding** this week to replace a "junk food" habit with an enriching one?

CHAPTER 18
The Shepherd's Time: Why Quantity and Quality Both Matter

A previous chapter established that the effective father-shepherd must be **present and engaged in the dark valleys** to guide our families. The question, however, is: how present? To answer that question adequately, we must confront a dangerous notion: the idea that "**quality over quantity**" is an acceptable standard for fathering. This mantra is rarely, if ever, applied to mothering, suggesting that the shepherd's daily presence and time are somehow less vital to the well-being of the flock than the mother's. I couldn't disagree more strongly.

While it is true that in many families today, the dad is the primary breadwinner, separating him from his children for many hours a day, the simple truth remains: **the more time he can spend with his children, the better.** Each moment is precious. This is particularly crucial considering the many hazards for children in the modern world. Mothers were not meant to bear the parenting load alone.

I understand the impulse to use the "quality over quantity" idea to make a father feel less guilty about time away from his child. However, this reasoning risks creating the notion that prioritizing **quantity** is not necessary when, in fact, it is essential. Yes, **quality** matters greatly. So does **quantity!** It is not a binary choice. For the dedicated shepherd, the objective is to strive for **both quality and quantity**.

A Brief History of the Wandering Shepherd

How did we arrive at a place where a father's time is seen as optional or easily substituted? The **Industrial Revolution** brought about dramatic changes that fundamentally altered the family unit, mainly for the worse, and fundamentally changed the role of the father-shepherd.

Shifting Roles and Family Dynamics

The shift from the family farm to the industrial factory floor was devastating to the shepherd's role:

- **Fathers Became Distant Breadwinners:** Traditionally involved in both work (on the farm) and family life (near the home), fathers became wage-earners working long hours away from the house. This led to **less time spent with children** and turned the father into a more distant, often authoritarian figure, whose primary role was financial provision rather than daily guidance.

- **Work and Home Separation:** With work removed from the home, a clear, damaging distinction between family life and labor was established. This led to a **loss of shared activities and traditions** that previously bound the shepherd and his flock together, robbing fathers of countless moments of teaching and bonding.

- **The Loss of Mentorship:** Consider the shepherd's role on the family farm, as was true in my father's early life in

Lowndes County, Alabama. He worked in the field, and on non-school days, his older children worked alongside him. This **proximity** provided ample opportunity for father-child bonding, practical teaching moments, and behavior modeling. When my father moved our family to Dayton, Ohio, to find better work, he began working long hours away from home, sometimes holding two jobs. Like many fathers of that era, he saw much less of his children. His dedication was heroic, especially since he lacked a role model due to his own father's abandonment. But the separation from the children was a significant change.

The historical societal shift contributed significantly to the tragic increase in fatherlessness and the modern acceptance of the "part-time" father—a wandering shepherd.

The Goal: Quality *And* Quantity

Children need **both** the devoted presence of the shepherd and the meaningful activities that deepen their connection. Quantity is relative and dependent upon a father's circumstances, but the principle is absolute.

For the father who works a standard schedule and has evenings and weekends available, strong fathering requires **prioritizing spending as much of that time as possible with his family (quantity)**. Less essential activities—such as personal hobbies, over-involvement in non-family commitments, or excessive overtime—should be secondary to the needs of the flock. Prioritizing family may mean turning down overtime, recognizing that the long-term emotional and spiritual wealth of the family outweighs short-term financial gain.

Quality could look like **planning meaningful time** with the whole family, date nights with the spouse, as well as one-on-one time with each child.

For a **non-custodial dad**, the challenge is intensified. Your quantity of parenting time may be limited to a few hours on a Saturday, every other weekend, or a few weeks in the summer. Your charge is to define what **quantity** and **quality** are possible for you in your unique circumstances. Use every communication tool available to increase the quantity of interaction.

Child-Parent Communication and Connection Tools

These tools help a noncustodial father stay connected to the child's daily life and maintain an intimate relationship, particularly beneficial for long-distance parenting.

Real-Time Video Calls (Virtual Visitation)

- **Common Examples:** FaceTime, Zoom, Google Meet, Skype

- **How to Maximize Parenting:** Have regular, scheduled **"virtual visits."** Use the visual element to engage in shared activities like reading bedtime stories, assisting with homework, or eating a meal together.

Messaging & Quick Check-ins

- **Common Examples:** Texting (SMS), WhatsApp, Snapchat (for older kids)

- **How to Maximize Parenting:** Send quick, **non-intrusive messages** about their day, wish them luck on a test/game, or send funny pictures/memes. Regular, small communication can maintain presence.

Shared Activities/Gaming

- **Common Examples:** Online Multiplayer Games, Shared Apps/Challenges

- **How to Maximize Parenting:** Play games together online. This creates **shared experiences** and gives you a non-pressured way to interact and talk while bonding over a fun activity.

Media Sharing

- **Common Examples:** Shared Photo Albums (Google Photos, Dropbox), Private Social Media Groups

- **How to Maximize Parenting:** Share photos and videos of your life and encourage the child to share theirs. This keeps you updated on events you missed and helps the child feel their life is important to you.

Asynchronous Communication

- **Common Examples:** Email, Recorded Video Messages

- **How to Maximize Parenting:** Send longer, more thoughtful emails or pre-recorded videos to share thoughts, stories, or encouragement, allowing the child to **respond when it's convenient** for them.

Making Every Moment Matter: Tending to the Sheep

Every moment a shepherd spends with his flock is a potential memory-making moment, a teaching opportunity, or a chance to deepen the bond. The key is to **be fully present** within that time. Choose activities that align with your child's age and interests and always focus on connection.

Ideas for Attentive Shepherding

Creative & Playful

- **Example Activities:** Build a fort; craft puppets and stage a show; paint masterpieces together; have a silly dance party.

- **The Shepherd's Role:** The **Engaged Guide** — You enter their world of imagination, validating their creativity and innocence.

Active & Adventurous

- **Example Activities:** Explore nature (hike, bike ride); build a birdhouse; play sports; volunteer together at a local charity.

- **The Shepherd's Role:** The **Protective Leader** — You model diligence, responsibility, and physical health while exploring the world safely.

Chill & Connect

- **Example Activities:** Read a book together; cook a meal together; stargaze; have a board game or puzzle night.

- **The Shepherd's Role:** The **Intimate Counselor** — You create space for quiet conversation, modeling cooperation and providing comfort.

Remember the key to quality time: **Focus on quality.** No matter the activity, give your child your full attention and **be present** in the moment. Be flexible, embrace their spontaneous ideas, and always **make it fun!**

Action: Prioritizing and Planning Shepherding Time

The shepherd's commitment to his flock should be intentional, not left to chance.

1. **Schedule It: Treat dad-child time like any other necessary appointment.** Block off time in your calendar and stick to it. This ensures you're making time for your kids, even when life gets busy.

2. **Be Present:** When you're with your kids, put away your phone and other distractions. Be **fully engaged** in what they're doing.

3. **Make It a Two-Way Street: Ask your kids what they want to do together.** Let them choose the activities and take the lead sometimes. This validates their voice and shows them you value their input.

4. **Be Consistent:** Try to make dad-child time a **regular part of your routine**. Even if it's just 30 minutes a day, making time for your kids regularly shows them that you care. Remember: kids spell love **T-I-M-E**.

5. **Cherish Every Moment:** Be yourself. Your kids don't need you to be perfect. They need you to be present, relaxed, and enjoy being their dad.

Guidance from the Holy Scriptures: A Command for Constant Presence

The Bible commands a constant, high-quantity presence in guiding children. The instructions God gave His ancient people are a perfect blueprint for the father-shepherd:

"Hear, O Israel: The Lord our God, the Lord is one! You shall love the Lord your God with all your heart, with all your soul, and with all your strength. And these words which I command you today shall be in your heart.

You shall teach them diligently to your children, and shall talk of them when you sit in your house, when you walk by the way, when you lie down, and when you rise up." — Deuteronomy 6:4-7 (NKJV)

This passage demands that teaching and connection occur at all times—whether sitting, walking, lying down, or rising. This is the biblical mandate for **quantity**—an unending, pervasive presence—ensuring that every moment is a **quality** opportunity for instruction and love. The shepherd is called to be inseparable from the flock he is charged to guide.

Questions for Reflection and Discussion

Quality and Quantity: The Biblical Mandate

- **The Binary Fallacy:** The chapter argues that "quality over quantity" is a dangerous notion that risks creating the idea that prioritizing quantity is not necessary. Do you find yourself using the "quality over quantity" mantra? If so, what **guilt or circumstance** does that phrase help you rationalize, and how can you instead commit to striving for **both** intentionality and time?

- **Constant Presence (Deuteronomy 6:4-7):** The Scripture commands teaching and connection to occur at all times — **when you sit, when you walk, when you lie down, and when you rise up.**

    - How well does your current routine reflect this **unending, pervasive presence**?

    - What is one practical adjustment you can make to turn a mundane, routine daily moment (like driving to school or sitting at the dinner table) into a moment of intentional teaching or bonding?

- **The Cost of Overtime:** Prioritizing family may mean turning down overtime or less essential activities. When considering taking on extra work or a personal hobby that consumes evenings, how do you measure the **long-term emotional and spiritual wealth** of your family against the short-term financial gain or personal fulfillment?

The Wandering Shepherd and Modern Tools

- **The Historical Shift:** The Industrial Revolution created a damaging separation between **work and home**, turning the father into a distant breadwinner. How are you actively working to **re-integrate** your children into your work or daily labor (e.g., showing them what you do, having them help with chores, explaining your challenges) to increase shared activity and mentorship?

- **The Non-Custodial Father:** If you are a non-custodial dad, your quantity of time is severely limited. Which **Child-Parent Communication Tool** (e.g., real-time video, shared gaming, asynchronous messages) can you commit to using **three times a week** to maintain a consistent, intimate presence in your child's daily life?

- **Making It a Two-Way Street: Making it fun** and letting your kids choose the activities is key to quality time. When planning your next dedicated time with your child, how will you ensure that **their interests and spontaneous ideas** take precedence over your planned agenda?

Prioritizing and Planning Shepherding Time

- **Schedule It and Be Consistent:** The shepherd's commitment must be **intentional, not left to chance**. Look at your calendar for the coming week. Have you blocked off a specific, dedicated block of "dad-child time," and what will you do to ensure you **stick to it** as a non-negotiable appointment?

- **The Quality Element:** Choose one idea from the **Attentive Shepherding** list (Creative & Playful, Active & Adventurous, or Chill & Connect). Plan to execute this activity this week, ensuring you **put away your phone and distractions** to give your child your full, undivided attention.

- **The Father's Identity:** The chapter reminds us: **"Kids spell love T-I-M-E."** What is the core message of love and presence you want your child to internalize from the amount and intentionality of the time you spend with them today?

*Considering the demands of your schedule, where can you create an extra 30 minutes of intentional, distraction-free **quality and quantity** time with your child this week?*

SECTION III - THE SHEPHERD AS SERVANT LEADER

CHAPTER 19
Guiding with a Towel, Not a Scepter

Having established the need for the father-shepherd's **full presence** and his commitment to both **quantity and quality** of time, we now turn to the **manner** in which he leads. The father is the head of his house, but this is a call to service, not a coronation. The most effective shepherd leads not from a position of detached superiority but with the **humility and sacrifice of a servant**.

Strong, servant-minded fathers are the greatest asset to their families and communities. The positive impact you can have on building a better world for families and children cannot be overstated. But all true transformation begins within the boundaries of the flock — it starts at home. This chapter focuses on how you, the father-shepherd, can adopt the mantle of **servant leadership** to optimize your guidance and build a thriving, secure household.

Defining the Family Shepherd's Servant Leadership

The idea that being the head of the house grants one a position of superiority to be wielded like a sledgehammer is a profound misunderstanding of biblical leadership. This does not end well. A better understanding of the role of the family head is that of a **servant leader**.

Servant leadership is a philosophy and model of leadership that fundamentally **prioritizes the needs of the people being served**, putting them first and helping them to develop and perform at their highest potential. It is a person-centered approach, in stark contrast to the traditional, hierarchical model where the leader is at the top, issuing orders down a chain of command.

For the family shepherd, this model is not simply a business strategy; it is a **divine calling**. Your authority comes with the obligation to care for your flock.

Jesus' washing of His disciples' feet is a profound model of **servant leadership**, directly challenging worldly notions of power and greatness. This act provides a clear template for the father to lead his family with humility and by meeting their **needs**.

Jesus' Demonstration of Servant Leadership

The account of Jesus washing His disciples' feet (John 13:1-17) perfectly encapsulates servant leadership:

- **Radical Humility:** In first-century Jewish culture, washing guests' feet was the task of the lowest servant or even a slave, especially at a formal meal. By taking off his outer garments, wrapping himself with a towel, and kneeling to perform this act, Jesus—their **Lord and Teacher**—intentionally took the position of the lowest servant. He did this even for **Judas**, who He knew was about to betray Him. This demonstrated that **no task or person is beneath a true leader**.

- **Action Over Status:** The disciples had just been arguing about which of them was the greatest (Luke 22:24). Jesus' action served as a powerful, non-verbal object lesson that **greatness in God's kingdom is measured by service**, not by position or authority.

- **Setting an Example:** Jesus explicitly told them, "I have set you an example that you should do as I have done for you" (John 13:15). He didn't just command service; He **modeled** it, showing them how to love and serve one another.

- **Meeting a Practical Need:** Beyond the spiritual lesson, He met a real, physical need. Their feet were dusty and dirty from the road, and this act provided essential cleansing and comfort.

The Family Shepherd's Call to Humility and Service

The father, as the family's shepherd, is called to lead his family in the same spirit, prioritizing the welfare of his wife and children over his own comfort or ego.

Leading with Humility

The foot-washing model teaches the family shepherd to lead from a position of **lowly service**, not lordly dominance:

- **Humble Example:** Like Jesus, the father should not wait for others to fill the most undesirable roles. Leading with humility means being the first to **serve in the small, often unseen ways** — doing the dirty work, getting up early, or taking on the tasks that no one wants to do, which can include chores, difficult conversations, or extending forgiveness.

- **Prioritizing Others:** Humility demands that the father "do nothing out of selfish ambition or vain conceit, but in humility value others above yourselves, not looking to your own interests but each of you to the interests of the others" (Philippians 2:3-4). This means **setting aside his own personal preferences or ego** for the greater good and harmony of the family.

- **Vulnerability and Apology:** A truly humble leader is secure enough to **admit when he is wrong** and to ask his wife and children for forgiveness. This vulnerability fosters a culture of grace and honesty in the home.

Key Characteristics of the Servant Shepherd:

- **Emphasis on Service:** The shepherd-leader sees his role as being of service to his family, not as a position of power over them.

- **Empathy:** He can put himself in the shoes of his children and wife, truly understanding their needs and feelings.

- **Listening:** He is a careful listener who makes time to hear the bleats, cries, and triumphs of his flock.

- **Humility:** He is humble and doesn't see himself as being above the mundane, everyday tasks required to care for the fold.

- **Stewardship:** He acts as a careful steward of his family's well-being and is committed to their long-term spiritual and emotional success.

- **Empowerment:** He empowers his wife and children to make decisions and take responsibility appropriate to their maturity.

- **Growth:** He is committed to the personal and spiritual growth of every member of his family.

Core Principles in Action: Leading the Household Flock

God created the first man, Adam, and placed him as the head of his family to love, lead, and **serve them**. Servant leadership of the family is a great privilege and a profound responsibility. The shepherd-leader fosters a happy and thriving family environment by applying these principles daily:

- **Empathy and Understanding:** Put yourself in the shoes of each family member. **Actively listen** to their concerns and communicate with open, honest vulnerability.

- **Empowerment and Autonomy:** Encourage your family members to take ownership. Delegate chores and responsibilities based on age and ability, providing guidance but allowing room for independent learning and growth. The flock must learn to graze and navigate the field safely on its own.

- **Growth and Development:** Foster a supportive environment where everyone feels encouraged to learn and reach their full potential. Provide opportunities for education, skill development, and character growth.

- **Collaboration and Teamwork:** Approach tasks and challenges as a team, working together toward common goals. Involve family members in decision-making processes and celebrate successes as a unified flock.

- **Humility and Service:** Be willing to **roll up your sleeves** and get involved in the everyday tasks of running the household. Prioritize the needs of the family above your own and **lead by example** through persistent acts of service.

Loving and Serving the Shepherd's Helper (Your Wife)

For the family shepherd, the relationship with the mother of his children is the **foundation of the whole fold**. Loving and serving her is the key to building a strong family. Women consistently tell me that it is not difficult for a wife to follow a husband who loves her, serves her well, and leads with honor. To build a stronger relationship, try **out-serving her**. Saying "I love you" is good, but **loving actions speak louder**.

The shepherd-leader applies his principles directly to his marriage:

Servant Shepherd Principles in Marriage

Empathy and Understanding

- **Practical Action:** Actively listen to her, giving your full attention. **Validate her emotions**, acknowledging her feelings even if you don't fully agree.

Empowerment and Autonomy

- **Practical Action:** Be an **equal partner** in chores and childcare, delegating tasks based on strengths. Support her personal and professional goals and **respect her judgment**.

Growth and Development

- **Practical Action:** Prioritize communication about your relationship and future. Be open to **feedback to grow together**. Encourage her hobbies and learning pursuits.

Humility and Service

- **Practical Action:** Be willing to **serve** by offering help with everyday tasks without being asked. Be ready to put her needs second and **apologize sincerely** when you make mistakes.

Remember: Your children are watching. They are observing how you serve their mother, and they are learning what true love, respect, and leadership look like.

Guiding your Lambs (Children)

Children do not primarily need a buddy; they need a **father** — a mature, responsible, loving, and nurturing adult male role model to shepherd them. Servant leadership in parenting is about creating a nurturing environment where your children feel loved, valued, and empowered to reach their potential.

Servant Shepherd Principles in Parenting

Empathy and Understanding

- **Practical Action:** Connect emotionally by getting down to their level . See the world through their eyes, considering their age and developmental stage. Embrace vulnerability by sharing appropriate emotions.

Empowerment and Autonomy

- **Practical Action:** Provide opportunities for **choice** (e.g., clothes, activities) within their capabilities. Encourage **healthy risk-taking** by allowing them to explore and learn from mistakes without hovering over them.

Growth and Development

- **Practical Action:** Be a lifelong learner yourself, **modeling curiosity**. Nurture their talents and interests by providing resources and celebrating achievements. Foster **critical thinking** by asking open-ended questions.

Collaboration and Teamwork

- **Practical Action:** Approach challenges as a **team**, valuing their input on family decisions. Hold a simple **family council (meeting)** where everyone can discuss issues and ideas.

Humility and Service

- **Practical Action:** Model **humility and forgiveness** by admitting your mistakes and **apologizing sincerely**. Be willing to help with everyday tasks (chores) and make sacrifices to ensure their well-being.

Servant leadership is a journey, not a destination. It's about building a strong foundation of trust, respect, and collaboration within the fold. By consistently applying these principles, you create a nurturing environment where every sheep and lamb feels valued, empowered, and supported to thrive.

Inspiration from the Holy Scriptures

The ultimate example of the shepherd's servant heart is found in the compassion modeled by God Himself. This is the quality to which every father is called:

*"As a father has **compassion** on his children, so the Lord has compassion on those who fear him."* — Psalm 103:13

Your call as a shepherd is to lead with this divine **compassion**, prioritizing service over status and humility over pride. Lead by serving, and you will lead well.

Questions for Reflection and Discussion

Defining Servant Leadership

- **Scepter vs. Towel:** The chapter contrasts leading with a **scepter** (lordly dominance) versus a **towel** (lowly service). In what small, everyday ways have you recently been tempted to lead with a **scepter** (demanding obedience or comfort) rather than a **towel** (humble service or difficult tasks)?

- **Radical Humility (John 13:1-17):** Jesus took the position of the lowest servant. What is one specific, undesirable task or chore in your household that you typically leave for your parenting partner or children, but which you can commit to **taking on yourself** this week as an act of radical humility and service?

- **Vulnerability and Apology:** A humble leader is secure enough to admit fault and ask for forgiveness. When was the last time you offered a **sincere, specific apology** to your spouse or child, and how did that act of vulnerability affect the culture of grace and honesty in your home?

The Servant Shepherd in Action

- **Prioritizing Others (Philippians 2:3-4):** Humility demands valuing **"others above yourselves, not looking to your own interests."** Identify one personal preference, hobby, or comfort that you can willingly set aside or defer this week to prioritize the greater good, harmony, or specific need of your family.

- **Empathy and Listening:** The servant shepherd is a careful listener who makes time to hear the **"bleats, cries, and triumphs"** of his flock. What is the one emotional state (sadness, anger, frustration, or fear) that your child or spouse expresses that you find the **most difficult** to empathize with, and how can you change your initial reaction to be more validating and understanding?

- **Empowerment in Parenting:** Servant leadership is about **empowerment and autonomy.** How are you providing opportunities for your children to take **healthy risks** and learn from their mistakes, rather than simply hovering over them or taking control of tasks you know you can do better?

Foundation of the Fold (Serving Your Wife)

- **Modeling for Your Children:** Your children are watching how you serve their mother. If your children were asked to describe what **true love, respect, and leadership** look like based on how you treat their mother, what three words would they use? Do those words reflect the principles of the **Servant Shepherd**?

- **Out-Serving Your Partner:** The chapter suggests trying to **out-serve your partner.** What is one **practical action** (e.g., taking the kids out so she can have quiet time, doing a necessary chore without being asked) that you can perform this week to model the principle of **Humility and Service** in your marriage?

- **Divine Compassion (Psalm 103:13):** The ultimate inspiration is the Lord's compassion. How does actively choosing to lead with **divine compassion** — prioritizing service over status—change the way you respond when your spouse or child makes a mistake?

CHAPTER 20
Discipline that Nurtures: Tending Your Flock with Love

Wise parents agree that children—our precious **flock**—need guidance and support. Guidance includes disciplining. The question for the **family shepherd** is: What is **effective, nurturing discipline?**

The true meaning of discipline is not punishment; it is **teaching and training.** It is the shepherd's staff, used to **guide the lamb** onto the right path, not merely to strike it for straying. It is about shaping behavior, not simply punishing wrongdoing.

We've all seen the frustrated parent trying to manage an unruly child in public. The embarrassment boils up, leading to yelling or harsh words. This is often the result of failing to consistently and lovingly tend the flock at home. I confess that early in my time as a shepherd of my oldest child—my young **lamb**—I resorted to a stern "talk" that was far from calm. Although the immediate behavior stopped, I realized I had failed to apply the more effective guidance and training methods at home. The key is to develop good, consistent parental discipline and then trust the foundation you've built.

The Shepherd's Keys to Guiding the Flock

Parental discipline is the process by which parents teach their children the appropriate behavior and the values of the home. It involves setting up the fences (boundaries), providing direction (guidance), and teaching the lambs to choose the greenest pastures (making responsible choices). This guidance must be based on **love, respect, and open communication.**[xiii]

1. Clear Fences and Pastures (Set Clear Expectations)

A good shepherd ensures his flock knows the boundaries.

- **Communicate Clearly:** Tell your **lambs** what is expected. Use simple, clear language to explain the rules.

- **Be Consistent:** Apply the rules faithfully. When the rules are consistent, the **flock feels secure** and is less confused.

2. Treats and Rest (Provide Positive Reinforcement)

The **shepherd** rewards good behavior to encourage more of it.

- **Praise the Good Walk:** Make a big deal when your **lamb** follows directions or does the right thing. Children crave the encouraging pats and cheers from their father. **You will get more of what you praise.**

- **Reward Effort:** Notice when your child is well-behaved, perhaps rewarding that **lamb** with a small, healthy reinforcer for choosing to stay near the path.

3. Feeling the Thistle (Use Natural Consequences)

Allow your children to experience the **natural consequences** of straying.

- **Learning from Pain:** It can be hard for the **shepherd** to watch, but the discomfort felt when a **lamb** suffers a consequence is a powerful teacher.

- **Example:** If a child neglects to pack their own backpack, the consequence might be forgetting a needed item at school.

4. The Gentle Staff (Avoiding Physical Punishment)

The **shepherd's staff** is for guidance, not abuse.

- **Kindness is Power:** You will find that harsh or **physical punishment is unnecessary** when loving, nurturing methods are consistently used in training the **lambs**.

- **Promote Open Communication:** Create a safe space for your **lambs** to express their feelings. Listen to their perspective and use gentle, respectful words.[xiv]

5. Modeling the Path (Guidance and Support)

The **shepherd** leads by example.

- **Offer Choices:** Give your **lambs** options within the safe boundaries you've set. This empowers them to practice responsible decision-making.

- **Model Calm:** Stay calm and assertive to **avoid power struggles**. Children learn how to regulate their own emotions by watching you manage yours.

Love: The Shepherd's Heart

The cornerstone of your work as the **family shepherd** is **love** — the Greek word *agape*. This is the same powerful, patient love God has for us, his own flock.[xv]

The characteristics of this love — **patience and kindness** — are the essential traits of a good shepherd. Training a child requires deep patience, allowing the father to be more tolerant of his children's repeated aggravations. Kindness means avoiding harsh words and attitudes when guiding the **lambs**.

Love is the safe enclosure where children feel valued and secure. When the **flock** feels loved, they are more likely to:

- **Trust the Shepherd:** This encourages open communication and cooperation.

- **Stay within Boundaries:** They respect the rules because they understand the boundaries come from a place of care and protection.

- **Develop Self-Worth:** A loved **lamb** is a confident **lamb** with a positive self-image.

In conclusion, fathers, you are called to provide loving masculine **nurturance** as you train your **flock**. Ultimately, **discipline in love** helps your **lambs** develop into well-adjusted individuals, capable of forming healthy relationships and exhibiting responsible behavior, and prepared for the journey ahead.

Instruction from the Holy Scriptures: *Train up a child in the way he should go, And when he is old he will not depart from it.* – **Proverbs 22:6**

Questions for Reflection and Discussion

Discipline: Teaching and Training

- **Discipline vs. Punishment:** The chapter states that the true meaning of discipline is **teaching and training**, not punishment. When your child misbehaves, is your immediate, instinctive response focused more on **stopping the behavior immediately** (punishment) or on **using the moment to teach a better skill or value** (training)? How can you shift your focus to training?

- **The Shepherd's Staff:** The staff is used to **guide the lamb onto the right path**, not to strike it. Describe a recent instance of misbehavior where you used your "staff" to guide and correct your child gently, and what was the long-term lesson you focused on teaching, beyond the immediate consequence?

- **Modeling Calm:** The shepherd leads by example, needing to **model calm** to teach children how to regulate their emotions. If you find yourself getting frustrated or yelling, what is one **proactive strategy** you can use (e.g., counting to ten, taking a deep breath, leaving the room briefly) to manage your own emotions before responding to your child?

The Shepherd's Keys to Guiding the Flock

- **Key #1: Clear Fences and Pastures: Consistency** in applying rules is essential for the flock to feel secure. Identify one family rule or boundary that you and your parenting partner have been **inconsistent** about recently. What specific action will you take *together* this week to re-establish and consistently enforce that rule?

- **Key #2: Treats and Rest (Positive Reinforcement):** The shepherd gets more of what he praises. When was the last time you made a **"big deal"** about a small act of positive behavior (e.g., following directions without prompting, showing kindness to a sibling)? Commit to delivering two specific, genuine compliments to your children today that praise their **effort** or **positive choices**.

- **Key #3: Feeling the Thistle (Natural Consequences):** Allowing your child to feel the **natural consequences** of straying is a powerful teacher. Describe a current situation where you are tempted to **rescue** your child from a consequence (e.g., completing homework they forgot, replacing a lost item). How will you allow them to experience the "thistle" instead, and what is the lesson you want them to learn?

- **Key #4: The Gentle Staff (Avoiding Physical Punishment):** Kindness is power and promotes open communication. How can you ensure that you are consistently creating a **safe space** for your children to express their feelings without fear of harsh words or attitudes from you?

Love: The Shepherd's Heart

- **Agape Love:** The cornerstone of shepherding is **agape love** (patient, kind). Which characteristic of *agape* love — **patience** (tolerance of repeated aggravations) or **kindness** (avoiding harsh words) — do you most need to focus on developing in your parenting this week?

- **Training for the Journey (Proverbs 22:6):** "Train up a child in the way he should go, and when he is old he

will not depart from it." What is the "way he should go" (the core value or belief) that you are diligently focusing on teaching and training your children right now, so that it becomes a permanent part of their character?

CHAPTER 21
Shepherding the Strong-Willed Child: Guiding the Headstrong Lamb

"You are hard-headed!" the parent yells, utterly defeated. Have you been there? Perhaps not screaming, but feeling that deep, soul-shaking frustration? Trying to guide a stubborn, defiant, strong-willed lamb that acts more like a **goat** can be absolutely exhausting.

The good news is that the "negative" energy behind strong-willed behavior is pure gold. With proper guidance, that defiance channels into powerful adult traits like **persistence, determination, and assertiveness.** The secret for the **family shepherd** isn't to break the child's strong will, but to **guide it constructively.** This task of reframing is challenging, but the reward — a confident, capable adult — is worth the effort.

First, let's define the **headstrong lamb** we are talking about.

"Strong-willed" is a spectrum of characteristics that, when viewed correctly (reframed with an asset-based viewpoint), are assets waiting to be cultivated. Doing so keeps with the scriptural instruction to *"train up a child in the way he should go..."* (Proverbs 22:6).

REFRAMING DEFIANT BEHAVIOR

Stubbornness / Refusal to Quit

- **Shepherd's Reframing (The Asset): Determination and Persistence** — Unwavering focus on achieving goals.

Arguing / Strong Opinions

- **Shepherd's Reframing (The Asset): Independent Thinking** — Clear ideas and the courage to express them.

Defiance / Standing Up to You

- **Shepherd's Reframing (The Asset): Assertiveness and Leadership** — Comfortable standing up for themselves and their beliefs.

Questioning Every Rule

- **Shepherd's Reframing (The Asset): Seeking Understanding** — A need to comprehend rules and a strong sense of justice.

Strong, Intense Reactions

- **Shepherd's Reframing (The Asset): Emotional Intensity** — Experiences emotions deeply, showing great passion in all things.

"Selective Hearing"

- **Shepherd's Reframing (The Asset): Independence** — Wants to do things their own way and resists following instructions they disagree with.

It's crucial to understand that these traits are not inherently harmful. They are simply powerful energy awaiting the shepherd's gentle hand to direct them.

Why Harsh Discipline Fails the Strong-Willed Child

The **headstrong lamb** will naturally resist being forced. As the **shepherd**, you must realize that harsh punishment — screaming, intimidation, or physical force — is generally ineffective and counterproductive for this type of child:

- **It Fuels Power Struggles:** Strong-willed children crave control. Harsh tactics intensify this need, causing them to dig in their heels and increase defiance rather than comply.

- **It Damages Trust:** Harshness erodes the parent-child relationship, replacing trust with resentment and fear. A strong, positive bond is the only tool that allows a shepherd to guide truly.

- **It Doesn't Teach Self-Control:** Punishment relies on fear, not learning. Your child learns to avoid being caught, not how to manage their intense emotions or make better long-term choices.

- **It Creates Secrecy:** When children are harshly punished, they learn to hide their behaviors instead of correcting them. This leads to bigger problems down the line.

Seeing Beyond Today's Frustrations

Take heart, **shepherd**! The characteristics that make parenting difficult today are the same traits that lead to remarkable success tomorrow.

The headstrong **lamb** that relentlessly pursues a goal can become the adult entrepreneur or innovator who **overcomes obstacles and achieves significant accomplishments.** The child who questions your authority will likely become the innovative adult who **challenges the status quo** and drives positive change in the world. The child who naturally takes charge will develop into the leader who **inspires and motivates others.**

The key takeaway is this: You are not eliminating a child's strong will; you are guiding them to use it constructively.

Key Strategies for Shepherding the Strong-Willed

Your most effective strategies are centered on respecting their need for control while providing a firm, loving structure.

1. Understand and Reframe the Behavior

- **Recognize the Positive Core:** Reframe "stubbornness" as "determination" and "defiance" as **"leadership potential."** Shift your perspective from seeing their behavior as a personal challenge to seeing it as a need for control or understanding.

- **Understand the "Why":** Why is your **lamb** fighting this instruction? Are they seeking attention, feeling frustrated, or asserting their independence? Address the underlying need, not just the behavior.

2. Grant Controlled Power

- **Offer Choices and Control:** Strong-willed children crave control. Offer them choices within your established boundaries. For example, don't say, "Put on your pajamas now." Instead, ask, **"Do you want to put on the blue pajamas or the striped pajamas?"** This gives them a sense of autonomy.

- **Practice Active Listening:** Listen to their concerns and acknowledge their feelings. Show them that you respect their opinions, even when you must hold a firm boundary.

3. Maintain the Shepherd's Compass

- **Establish Clear and Consistent Boundaries:** Children thrive on a reliable structure. Set clear rules and, when they are broken, follow through with consequences. **Consistency is your most powerful tool.**

- **Maintain Calmness:** Strong-willed children will push your buttons like no one else. Try to **remain calm** and avoid entering a power struggle. When you model self-control, you teach them self-regulation.

- **Focus on Positive Reinforcement: Catch them doing good** and praise their positive behavior. A simple word of encouragement is more effective than constant criticism.

4. Build the Strong Connection

- **Nurture the Relationship:** Spend **quality time** together and show them unconditional love. A strong connection makes your guidance ten times more effective.

- **Teach Problem-Solving:** Help your child learn how to manage conflicts and their intense emotions. Guide them through identifying a problem, brainstorming solutions, and evaluating the outcomes.

Instructions From the Holy Scriptures

As you face the daily challenges of guiding your strong-willed child, remember the foundation of your faith:

*Love is **patient**, love is **kind**…* - **1 Corinthians 13:4** (NIV)

Patience and kindness are the essential tools for the shepherd guiding the headstrong lamb.

Questions for Reflection and Discussion

Reframing Defiant Behavior

- **The Gold in the Defiance:** The chapter asserts that the "negative" energy of a strong-willed child is **"pure gold"** that channels into traits like **persistence and assertiveness**. Identify one challenging behavior in your child (e.g., arguing, refusal to quit). How can you practice **reframing** that behavior today, seeing it as an asset (e.g., Independent Thinking, Determination) rather than a personal challenge?

- **Seeing Beyond Frustration:** The characteristics that make parenting difficult today are the same traits that lead to **remarkable success tomorrow** (e.g., entrepreneur, innovator). What is your biggest current frustration with your child's strong will, and how does focusing on their **future success** (the confident, capable adult) help you remain patient in this difficult moment?

- **Seeking Understanding:** Strong-willed children often exhibit **"Questioning Every Rule"** because they have a strong **sense of justice** and need to understand. When your child questions a rule, do you usually shut down the discussion or enter into a dialogue? How can you show respect for their **seeking understanding** while still maintaining the final boundary?

Why Harsh Discipline Fails

- **Fueling Power Struggles:** Harsh tactics intensify the strong-willed child's **craving for control**. Describe a recent power struggle you had. What part did your **harsh** or **forceful response** play in causing your child to "dig in their heels" and continue the defiance?

- **Damaging Trust:** Harshness damages the parent-child relationship, replacing trust with **resentment and fear.** Why is a **strong, positive bond** the *only* effective tool for guiding a child who naturally resists being forced?

- **Creating Secrecy:** When children are harshly punished, they learn to **hide their behaviors.** What is one way you can immediately foster a stronger connection so that your child feels safe to admit missteps rather than hiding their actions out of fear of your reaction?

Key Strategies for Shepherding

- **Granting Controlled Power:** Strong-willed children crave **control.** What is one simple area of routine (e.g., getting dressed, bedtime, choosing a snack) where you can begin to consistently **offer choices** within your established boundaries ("Do you want A or B?") to grant them a sense of autonomy?

- **Maintain the Shepherd's Compass: Consistency** and **Calmness** are your most powerful tools. Which one is harder for you to maintain when faced with defiance? What is your **"emergency" plan** (mental or physical) for remaining calm and avoiding entering a power struggle the next time your child pushes your buttons?

- **Build the Strong Connection:** A strong connection makes guidance ten times more effective. What is one way you can commit to **spending quality time** this week to nurture the relationship and demonstrate unconditional love, even if their behavior is currently challenging?

- **Patience and Kindness (1 Corinthians 13:4):** As you face the daily challenge of guiding your headstrong lamb, why are **patience and kindness** the foundational tools, and how does your faith empower you to apply them when you feel exhausted?

SECTION IV – SHEPHERDING UNDER STRESS

CHAPTER 22
Battling Despair: Encouragement for Struggling Shepherds

It's tough being a dad. For the **family shepherd**—the father who commits his strength and heart to serve his **flock**—feelings of inadequacy and despair can be a heavy, draining burden. If you've felt discouraged, know you are not alone. These feelings are common, real, and worth fighting. This section of *The Family Shepherd* serves as your rallying cry, outlining the causes of discouragement and stress and providing battle-tested strategies to overcome with the help of the Divine Shepherd.

Sources of the Shepherd's Struggle

Fatherhood, while immensely rewarding, presents challenges that, day by day, can chip away at your emotional well-being. Do you recognize any of these common burdens?

The Burden of Unrealistic Expectations

- **The Myth of the Perfect Provider:** You feel pressure to be the primary provider, the strong protector, the always-involved parent, and the skilled handyman—all at once. This **unrealistic combination** leads to feelings of inadequacy and failure.

- **The Comparison Trap:** Browsing social media or observing other families can make you feel like you aren't measuring up as a father.

- **The Time Tug-of-War:** You worry about not spending enough time with your children due to work, or feel unproductive at work due to family responsibilities, leaving you perpetually **exhausted and emotionally drained.**

Internal and Relational Stressors

- **Parenting Doubts:** You worry about making wrong decisions, not knowing how to handle difficult situations, or feeling like you aren't connecting with your children effectively as they grow.

- **Lack of Appreciation:** Not feeling recognized or appreciated for your constant efforts — the daily grind of providing and protecting — can lead to resentment and **deep despair.**

- **Isolation and Distance:** Work schedules, differing interests, or communication breakdowns can lead to feeling **isolated** from your children.

Overlooked Factors Affecting the Shepherd

- **Emotional and Mental Health:** Conditions like **paternal postpartum depression and anxiety** are real but often overlooked, severely impacting a father's mood and ability to cope.

- **Sleep Deprivation:** The disruption to sleep, especially with young children, impacts your energy and mood levels, making every task feel overwhelming.

- **Lack of Support:** The societal pressure to be **stoic** and not express vulnerability can lead to feelings of loneliness.

- **Specific Challenges:** Dealing with children's behavioral or developmental issues, or navigating **co-parenting after separation**, can be emotionally taxing and make you question your parenting abilities.

If you recognize these sources of discouragement, it's time to purposefully pursue strategies to restore your well-being. Addressing these issues benefits you, your children, and your entire family.

Strategies for Battling Discouragement

Waging war against discouragement requires an intentional commitment to **self-care, perspective, and connection.**

Prioritize Self-Care (The Shepherd Must Refuel)

- **It's Not Selfish:** Make time for activities that **recharge you,** even if it's just for a few minutes. When you're running on empty, everything feels harder.

- **Nourish Body and Mind: Eat healthy, hydrate, and prioritize sleep.** These basic needs have a massive impact on your mood and energy.

- **Exercise Regularly:** Physical activity is a fantastic **mood booster and stress reliever.** Even a short walk can make a difference.

- **Practice Mindfulness:** Techniques like deep breathing, meditation, or yoga help manage stress and quiet negative thoughts.

Shift Your Perspective (Reframing the View)

- **Focus on the Small Wins:** Parenthood is full of little victories. Acknowledge and celebrate those moments— did your child share a toy? Did you successfully navigate a tough conversation? **These things matter.**

- **Practice Gratitude:** Take a few moments daily to reflect on what you are grateful for. This simple act **shifts your focus** from what's going wrong to what's going well.

- **Challenge Negative Thoughts:** When you hear those discouraging thoughts, question them. **Are they really true?** Try to reframe them in a more positive or realistic light.

- **Embrace Imperfection:** No parent is perfect. It's okay. Learn from moments you feel you've failed, and **move forward.** Don't chase an unrealistic ideal.

Connect and Seek Support (Leaning on the Community)

- **Talk to Your Partner:** Share your feelings and challenges with your spouse. They can offer emotional support, a different perspective, and help you **share the load.**

- **Connect with Other Fathers:** Sharing experiences and knowing you're not alone is incredibly helpful. Consider using resources like the **Fathering Strong® app** to connect with other dads and share insights.

- **Seek Professional Help:** If feelings of discouragement persist, are overwhelming, or are impacting your daily life, please don't hesitate to reach out to a **therapist or counselor.**

Take Action (Changing the Path)

- **Set Realistic Expectations:** Be honest about what you can realistically accomplish in a day. **Don't try to do everything at once.**

- **Break Down Tasks:** Feeling overwhelmed leads to discouragement. Break down large, daunting tasks into **smaller, more manageable steps.**

- **Delegate and Ask for Help:** Don't try to shoulder all the responsibilities yourself. Delegate tasks to your partner or older children, and **don't be afraid to ask for help** when you need it.

- **Create Positive Family Rituals:** Simple, consistent quality time together strengthens your connection and boosts everyone's spirits.

Remember, battling discouragement is an **ongoing process.** Be patient with yourself, celebrate your progress, and trust in the loving work you are doing for your family.

Inspiration From Holy Scriptures

When you find yourself thinking discouraging or worrying thoughts, actively challenge them. **Replace them with positive, uplifting truths.** Turn your thoughts to God, your ultimate Shepherd, who offers strength and peace.

Summing it all up, friends, I'd say you'll do best by filling your minds and meditating on things true, noble, reputable, authentic, compelling, gracious — the best, not the worst; the beautiful, not the ugly; things to praise, not things to curse. Put into practice what you learned from me, what you heard and saw and realized. Do that, and God, who makes everything work together, will work you into his most excellent **harmonies**. - **Philippians 4:8-9 (The Message)**

"Be not dismayed, for I am your God. I will **strengthen you**, yes, I will **help you**…" – **Isaiah 41:10 (NKJV)**

Questions for Reflection and Discussion

Sources of the Shepherd's Struggle

- **The Comparison Trap:** The chapter identifies the **Comparison Trap** (often fueled by social media) as a source of inadequacy. What specific, external influence (social media feed, conversation with a neighbor, observation of another family) most often makes you feel like you are **not measuring up** as a father? What concrete step can you take to reduce your exposure to that influence?

- **The Time Tug-of-War:** Do you currently feel guilt about **not spending enough time with your children** due to work, or feeling **unproductive at work** due to family responsibilities? What is one minor, realistic adjustment you can make this week to lessen the tension of this tug-of-war?

- **Paternal Postpartum Depression and Anxiety:** The text notes that these conditions are real but often overlooked. In your community or among your peers, why is there frequently societal **pressure to be stoic** that prevents fathers from expressing vulnerability or seeking help for emotional and mental health struggles?

- **Lack of Appreciation:** Not feeling recognized for the daily grind of providing and protecting can lead to despair. What is the **one small, consistent action** (e.g., a kind word, a supportive touch, an acknowledgment of effort) that you most value from your partner, and have you clearly communicated this need to them?

Strategies for Battling Discouragement

- **Prioritize Self-Care (Refueling):** The family shepherd must refuel to fight effectively. Beyond getting better sleep, what is one **non-negotiable activity** that recharges you (physical, mental, or spiritual) that you will **schedule and protect** for at least 30 minutes this week?

- **Shift Your Perspective (Small Wins):** Discouragement thrives when we focus on failures. Name **two "small wins"** from your last 24 hours (e.g., successful navigation of a tough conversation, a moment of connection with a child, completing a necessary chore). How does acknowledging these small victories change your overall view of your fathering?

- **Connect and Seek Support:** Sharing experiences helps combat loneliness. What is the biggest challenge in your fathering right now, and which **trusted father or mentor** can you reach out to **this week** to share this burden with and seek insight from?

- **Take Action (Delegation):** The family shepherd should not try to shoulder all responsibilities. What is one household or parenting task that you can **delegate or ask for help with** this week to alleviate an area of overwhelm?

Inspiration From Holy Scriptures

- **Challenging Negative Thoughts (Philippians 4:8-9):** The Scripture advises filling your mind with things that are **"true, noble, reputable, authentic, compelling, gracious."** When a negative, self-defeating thought enters your mind (e.g., "I'm a failure as a dad"), what is the corresponding **truth or virtue** you can immediately use to replace or challenge that thought?

- **Divine Strength (Isaiah 41:10):** The Lord promises, **"Be not dismayed, for I am your God. I will strengthen you, yes, I will help you..."** How does placing your trust in the Divine Shepherd—who offers strength and peace—empower you to be more patient and effective as a shepherd to your own flock?

CHAPTER 23
The Shepherd in the Press: Protecting Your Flock from the Strains of Life

As stated earlier, the shepherd's life, much like the earthly father's, is not lived in a peaceful, manicured meadow. The world is a **pressure-filled landscape**, fraught with dangers both seen and unseen. When you couple the strains of simply living—of providing, protecting, and navigating a complex society—with the sacred duties of **marriage and raising children**, the weight can feel overwhelming. The constant tension of life can easily become a crushing burden, impacting your ability to tend your flock with the wisdom and compassion they deserve.

In this chapter, we will examine the **hazards of pressure** on your family and, crucially, offer practical strategies for the Christian father-shepherd to manage these challenges without cracking under the strain.

Understanding the Hazards: When the World Presses In

A good shepherd is always aware of the terrain and the potential threats to his sheep. Likewise, you must recognize the forces that conspire to wear you down and compromise your effectiveness as a father and husband.

Here are some of the most **Common Pressures on the Shepherd-Father:**

- **Financial Strain:** The constant worry of **provision**, whether it's the high cost of the necessities, childcare, healthcare, or job insecurity, can be a perpetual storm cloud over the sheepfold.

- **Time Demands and Exhaustion:** Juggling the demands of **work, home maintenance, and active fathering** leaves many shepherds utterly depleted. This is compounded by the **lack of sleep**, especially with infants or toddlers, a basic need often sacrificed on the altar of a busy life.

- **Behavioral Challenges:** The "straying" of the sheep, in the form of **children's behavioral issues**, tantrums, and the need for consistent discipline and boundary setting, can be a significant source of stress.

- **Societal Noise:** The ever-present **social and cultural pressures** to be a "perfect parent" or provide a picture-perfect life—often amplified by social media—creates an unrealistic burden.

- **Isolation:** The best shepherds know the importance of a community. **Lack of social support** can lead to parental isolation and loneliness, amplifying stress in the lonely watch.

- **Inner Turmoil:** A shepherd struggling with his own **mental health issues** (anxiety, depression) will find it exponentially harder to manage the demands of the flock.

When a shepherd is overwhelmed by these pressures, his ability to lead and nurture is severely diminished, leading to a cascade of negative consequences for his family.

The Dangers of a Strained Shepherd

A shepherd under poorly managed pressure is a danger to his flock. Do you recognize any of these impacts on yourself or your co-parent?

Impact on the Shepherd-Child Relationship

- **Weakened Bond:** Chronic stress makes a parent less emotionally available, like a shepherd who is present but too weary to attend to the needs of a struggling lamb.

- **Inconsistent Tending:** The stressed parent may swing wildly between being overly harsh and overly lax—a confusing and unpredictable environment for a developing child.

- **Harsh Words and Actions:** Pressure makes the shepherd prone to **snapping, yelling, or resorting to harsh discipline**, replacing patient guidance with frustrated reaction.

- **Reduced Quality Time:** The shepherd may lack the energy to **engage positively** with his children, limiting meaningful connection.

- **Negative Role Modeling:** Children learn how to handle stress by watching their parents. If the father's coping mechanism is anger, withdrawal, or constant anxiety, the child internalizes this unhealthy pattern.

- **Parental Burnout:** Prolonged, unmanaged stress leads to **burnout**, an emotional exhaustion that increases the risk of emotional distancing, neglect, or even anger toward the children.

Impact on the Lambs (Your Children)

The unmanaged stress of the parents casts a long shadow over the children, affecting their development and well-being:

- **Emotional and Behavioral Problems:** Children may develop **internalizing issues** (anxiety, withdrawal, low self-esteem) or **externalizing issues** (aggression, defiance).

- **Attachment Issues:** They may struggle to form **secure attachments**, leading to insecurity and difficulty in future relationships.

- **Developmental Stalling:** Stressed parents have less energy for stimulating activities, which are crucial for language acquisition and problem-solving. Furthermore, chronic stress can lead to **hypervigilance** in a child, making it difficult to focus on learning and academics.

- **Social Withdrawal:** Witnessing persistent parental conflict or stress can disrupt a child's social-emotional learning, leading to social difficulty.

- **Burden Bearing:** The most heartbreaking consequence is when children feel responsible for their parents' emotions, carrying a **burden beyond their years**.

These are serious issues. A wise shepherd must recognize the signs of a strained heart and actively seek solutions to address it.

Strategies for the Resilient Shepherd

To effectively care for your flock, you must first care for the shepherd. Here are key strategies for managing parental stress in healthy, sustainable ways.

1. Sharpen Your Tools: Prioritize Self-Care

A shepherd cannot pour life-giving water from an empty cup. **Self-care is not selfish; it is essential.**

- **Schedule "Me Time":** Put 10-15 minutes of quiet time, reading, or hobby pursuit in your calendar. Treat it as a non-negotiable appointment.

- **Prioritize Sleep:** This is the foundation of resilience. Establish and adhere to consistent sleep routines for yourself and your children.

- **Nourish and Move:** Maintain your physical strength by eating balanced meals and engaging in regular physical activity. Exercise is a natural stress reliever.

2. Build Your Support Flank

No shepherd should work alone. **"It takes a village"** is a timeless truth.

- **Connect with Fellow Shepherds:** Share experiences and advice with other fathers. Knowing you are not alone in the struggle is incredibly validating.

- **Lean on Family and Friends:** Do not be afraid to **ask for help** with childcare or household chores. **(This is why God created community.)**

- **Tend Your Marriage: Communicate openly with your partner.** Share the emotional load, discuss your feelings, and make time for your marital relationship actively. Your children feel the security of a strong parental bond.

3. Set Realistic Expectations

You cannot shepherd a perfect flock, because such a thing does not exist. **Let go of the illusion of perfection.**

- **Focus on Core Needs:** Prioritize your child's well-being and your family's fundamental, spiritual needs over striving for an "ideal" home or lifestyle.

- **Practice Self-Compassion:** Acknowledge that parenting is the hardest, most complex job in the world. Treat yourself with the same kindness and grace you would offer a struggling friend.

4. Establish Order and Boundaries

Routines reduce chaos, and clear boundaries protect your energy.

- **Consistent Routines:** Children thrive on predictability. Create consistent schedules for bedtimes and mealtimes to reduce daily friction.

- **Healthy Boundaries: It is okay to say "no"** to commitments that will overextend you. Protect your home and family time fiercely.

5. Seek Wisdom and Professional Counsel

- **Be a Student of Your Sheep:** Learn about **child development** and what is typical for your child's age. This knowledge reduces frustration and allows you to anticipate behaviors.

- **Know When to Call for a Specialist:** If you are consistently overwhelmed, anxious, or depressed, and your stress is harming your family, **seek help from a therapist or mental health professional.** Seeking help is a sign of strength and stewardship, not failure.

Instructions from the Holy Scriptures: Strength in the Press

The ultimate source of strength for the Christian shepherd comes from God. We are reminded of this in the words of the Apostle Paul:

We are hard-pressed on every side, yet not crushed; we are perplexed, but not in despair; persecuted, but not forsaken; struck down, but not destroyed. (2 Cor. 4:8-9)

You cannot escape the troubles of this world, but they do not have the power to destroy you or your family. God promises that while you will experience affliction, you are **not ultimately defeated**.

Turn all your stressors over to God in prayer and trust Him to give you the **peace of heart and mind** through Christ that *surpasses all understanding* (Phil. 4:6-8).

When Pressure Is a Good Thing: Lessons from the Olive Press

Believe it or not, the pressures of life and fathering, when managed with the help of the Holy Spirit, can serve a positive purpose.

While touring an ancient olive press in Israel with my wife, I learned that nothing is wasted in the oil-making process. The olives undergo a three-step pressing process to extract oil of varying qualities: first press, second press, and third press.

The olive press provides a powerful illustration for the Christian father:

- **Transformation:** Just as pressure extracts precious oil, the pressure in life can be a **catalyst for transformation and growth** in your character.

- **Resilience:** The olives are sturdy and can withstand pressure. As you lean on God, you develop the resilience to emerge stronger, more capable, and a better shepherd.

- **Focus:** The process forces the oil to separate from the pulp. Similarly, pressure in life helps us **focus on what truly matters**: our faith, our marriage, and the well-being of our children.

The takeaways are profound: **God doesn't waste our suffering.** He uses the pressures of life to make us better men, better husbands, and better fathers. He redeems the struggle because of our faith in Him.

Stay in the press. Keep faithfully serving God.

By actively adopting these strategies — prioritizing your self-care, building your support system, and anchoring your hope in Christ — you can navigate the pressures of raising children with greater resilience. This not only reduces stress on you but also creates a more positive and nurturing environment for your entire family.

Your faith is your greatest asset in this fight. Trust the Holy Spirit to assist you in managing stress by offering peace, strength, and guidance, ultimately fostering a deep sense of reliance on God, the Good Shepherd.

Questions for Reflection and Discussion

Understanding the Hazards of the Press

- **Identifying Your Pressure:** Of the Common Pressures listed (Financial Strain, Time Demands, Isolation, Inner Turmoil), which one currently feels like the **most crushing burden**? How is that specific pressure impacting your **emotional availability** to your children (Weakened Bond)?

- **Negative Role Modeling:** The chapter warns that children internalize the father's stress coping mechanisms (anger, withdrawal). What specific change in your behavior when stressed would provide your children with a **healthier role model** for handling pressure?

- **Inconsistent Tending:** A strained parent can swing between being **overly harsh and overly lax**. How does this inconsistency create a **confusing and unpredictable environment** for your developing child, particularly around discipline and boundaries?

- **The Weight of the Lambs:** The most heartbreaking consequence is when children feel like they are **burden-bearing** for your emotions. What cues (verbal or non-verbal) might you be giving off when overwhelmed that could lead your child to feel this responsibility?

Strategies for the Resilient Shepherd

- **Sharpening Your Tools (Self-Care):** Self-care is not selfish; it is essential. Have you scheduled and protected

10-15 minutes of non-negotiable **"Me Time"** in your calendar this week? What small, consistent physical action (Nourish and Move) can you start today to boost your mood and stress resilience?

- **Building Your Support Flank:** The shepherd needs community. What is **one specific, actionable item** (e.g., asking for help with a chore, sharing a struggle) that you can **Lean on Family and Friends** or **Connect with Fellow Shepherds** about this week?

- **Tend Your Marriage:** A strong parental bond is a source of security for the children. What is one **intentional act of communication** you will initiate with your partner this week to **share the emotional load** and actively reinforce your bond?

- **Setting Realistic Expectations:** What is one **illusion of perfection** (e.g., a flawless home, perfect behavior, ideal financial status) that you are willing to let go of this week to focus instead on your family's **Core Needs** (well-being and spiritual foundation)?

- **Seeking Professional Counsel:** Knowing that **seeking help is a sign of strength**, what initial research step can you take today to identify a therapist or counselor, should you need to reach out in the future?

Strength in the Press: The Spiritual View

- **The Olive Press Analogy (Transformation):** Just as pressure extracts precious oil, it refines your character. What **negative pressure** in your life right now can you reframe as a catalyst for developing a specific **positive character trait** (e.g., using financial strain to develop wisdom/discipline)?

- **Focus and Separation:** The pressing separates the oil from the pulp. What is the one non-essential activity or distraction (**the pulp**) that you need to eliminate or minimize to create more room for **what truly matters** (faith, marriage, children)?

- **Trusting the Promise (2 Cor. 4:8-9):** Meditate on the promise: **"hard-pressed... yet not crushed."** How does anchoring your hope in Christ—knowing you won't be ultimately destroyed by worldly stress—change the way you approach your biggest family challenge this week?

- **Peace that Surpasses Understanding (Phil. 4:6-8):** What is the **specific stressor** you will intentionally turn over to God in prayer this week, trusting Him to grant you peace instead of anxiety?

Disclaimer: This chapter offers scriptural guidance and is not a substitute for professional advice, diagnosis, or treatment. If you are experiencing significant stress or mental health concerns, please consult with a qualified healthcare provider.

CHAPTER 24
The Shepherd's Anchor: Managing Stress with the Power of Faith

In the previous chapter, we confronted some of the crushing **pressures of life and fatherhood**, recognizing the hazards they pose to the father-shepherd and his flock. Now, we turn to the most powerful resource available to the Christian man: the **strength and perspective found in faith**.

It is essential to understand that unmanaged stress is not merely a personal inconvenience; it is a **public health crisis** for families. Recent data from the U.S. confirms that parents are overwhelmingly burdened:

- **33% of parents** reported high stress levels in the past month (compared to 20% of other adults).

- **Nearly half (48%) of parents** reported that their stress is completely overwhelming on most days.

- **41% of parents** reported being so stressed they cannot function — **double** the rate of non-parents.

These alarming statistics are fueled by numerous factors, including financial strain (money worries consume 66% of parents), time demands, profound concerns about children's mental health and safety, and the cultural noise of **"perfect parenting"** promoted by technology and social media. The U.S. Surgeon General has rightly called for attention to this crisis of parental well-being.[xvi]

A Special Focus for the Family Shepherd

While mothers are also profoundly affected — and often disproportionately impacted by mental health conditions — we must address the specific challenge for fathers. Data consistently shows that **men are significantly less likely than women to seek professional counseling or mental health services.**[xvii]

This disparity is often rooted in:

- **Masculinity Stereotypes:** Men are often socialized to be **fiercely self-reliant**, viewing the need for help as a sign of weakness or a threat to their masculine identity. This creates a cultural barrier to seeking therapeutic support.

- **Emotional Suppression:** Many men are less willing to openly discuss emotions, preferring to **externalize problems** or rely on less healthy coping mechanisms, such as **substance abuse or isolation**, rather than engaging in introspective talk therapy.

For the father who bears the weight of provision and protection, this reluctance is a critical danger. If the shepherd refuses to mend his own wounds, the entire flock is vulnerable.

The good news is that the Christian faith offers a robust and accessible framework and toolset for stress management that aligns with the shepherd's need for strength, structure, and purpose. It is not a replacement for professional help when needed, but it is the unshakable foundation upon which all recovery and resilience are built.

Managing Stress Through the Power of Faith

The Christian faith provides the necessary **anchor** for the shepherd caught in the storms of life, offering a unique perspective and tangible spiritual practices to manage debilitating anxiety.

1. Trust in God's Sovereignty: The Ultimate Relief

The core principle that liberates the shepherd from crushing self-reliance is the conviction that **God is ultimately in control** (His **Sovereignty**). This belief enables you to:

- **Surrender Control:** Rather than feeling solely responsible for every unpredictable outcome, you can **surrender anxieties** to your Great Shepherd. This is the heart of the command:

"Do not be anxious about anything, but in every situation, by prayer and petition, with thanksgiving, present your requests to God. And the peace of God, which transcends all understanding, will guard your hearts and your minds in Christ Jesus" (Philippians 4:6-7 NIV).

- **Turn all the sources of your stress over to God, thankful that He cares (1 Pet. 5:7), and trusting that He will give you supernatural peace.**

- **Trust that even those things the enemy of your soul sends to harm you, God redeems for your good (Gen. 50:20).**

*Find Purpose in Pressure: You can view trials and stress not as meaningless suffering, but as **opportunities for spiritual growth** and* *character development. We know that "in all things God works for the good of those who love him, who have been called according to his purpose" (Romans 8:28).2.*

2. The Practical Tool of Prayer

Prayer is more than a spiritual sentiment; it is a practical mechanism for stress relief. It is the act of **"casting your cares upon Him"** (1 Peter 5:7).

- **Direct Communication:** Prayer allows you to express worries and fears, an act of verbalization that is incredibly liberating.

- **Finding Peace:** The very act of turning your focus from the immediate problem to **God's presence** can quiet the mind, leading to that profound peace that *"surpasses all understanding."*

3. Guidance from Scripture and Community

The Family Shepherd is not meant to wander alone. God has provided written **wisdom** and a **community** for support.

- **Renewing the Mind:** The Bible is a source of truth that counteracts the negative thought spirals of worry. We are commanded to *"be transformed by the renewing of your mind"* (Romans 12:2). This involves intentionally focusing your thoughts on *"whatever is true, whatever is noble, whatever is right, whatever is pure...think about such things"* (Philippians 4:8).

- **Bearing Burdens:** The Church community emphasizes *"carrying each other's burdens"* (Galatians 6:2). Connecting with fellow believers combats the **parental isolation** that amplifies stress, providing prayer, encouragement, and a powerful sense of belonging.

4. The Biblical Mandate for Rest and Compassion

Faith provides a framework for self-care, a concept often dismissed by stressed fathers.

- **Prioritize Rest:** The concept of the **Sabbath** (Exodus 20:8-10) is a biblical mandate for intentional **rest and renewal**. It reminds the shepherd that he is not God and is not designed to carry all his burdens alone.

- **Practice Forgiveness:** Unforgiveness and bitterness are heavy emotional burdens and significant sources of chronic stress. The emphasis on **forgiveness**, both for oneself and for others (Matthew 6:12, 14), releases the mind and heart from this crushing weight.

Summary and The Shepherd's Promise

The data confirms that the burden of stress on U.S. parents is acute. Especially for fathers who may resist professional help due to cultural pressures, the Christian faith provides a vital, powerful, and accessible avenue for relief.

Rather than being overwhelmed by the pressures of parenting, you are given a choice: **turn over every one of your cares and concerns to God in prayer.**

In thankfulness that He cares for you, ask Him to meet every need. As you do, you can **rest in confidence**. This is God's promise to His children: **the supernatural peace of God will protect your heart and mind from debilitating anxiety.**

Disclaimer: This chapter offers scriptural guidance and is not a substitute for professional advice, diagnosis, or treatment. If you are experiencing significant stress or mental health concerns, please consult with a qualified healthcare provider.

Questions for Reflection and Discussion

Confronting the Stress Crisis

- **The Burden of Fathers:** The data show that stress levels among parents are alarmingly high, with nearly half reporting feeling completely overwhelmed on most days. Does this statistical description accurately reflect the *average* feeling you carry regarding your fathering duties and financial provision? Why or why not?

- **Masculinity and Help-Seeking:** The chapter discusses the **cultural barrier** of masculinity stereotypes, which often leads men to view seeking professional help as a sign of weakness.

    - What is the **primary fear or belief** that would stop you from reaching out to a counselor or therapist during a period of acute stress or anxiety?

    - How can the church community and fellow fathers normalize the concept that **seeking professional help is an act of strength and responsible stewardship**?

- **The Shepherd's Wound:** The text states, "If the shepherd refuses to mend his own wounds, the entire flock is vulnerable." In what specific way does your current level of stress manifest itself (e.g., anger, impatience, silence) that makes your children and spouse **vulnerable**?

Managing Stress Through the Power of Faith

- **Trust in God's Sovereignty:** The core principle is surrendering control because **God is ultimately in control.** Identify one current, pressing worry about your children (safety, future, education) that you are struggling to manage alone. How can you intentionally **surrender this specific anxiety** to your Great Shepherd today?

- **Prayer as a Practical Tool:** Prayer is described as a practical mechanism for stress relief — the act of **verbalization** that is incredibly liberating. When you feel overwhelmed, is your first instinct to internalize/isolate or to pray and articulate your worries to God? What structure can you put in place to ensure prayer is your **default, immediate response?**

- **The Biblical Mandate for Rest (Sabbath):** The Sabbath is a mandate for intentional rest and renewal, reminding the shepherd that he is **not God.** Are you currently prioritizing a day or a designated time for deliberate rest and renewal? If not, what is the **greatest idol of busyness or performance** that is causing you to sacrifice this God-given rhythm?

- **Renewing the Mind (Philippians 4:8):** When you experience negative thought spirals of worry, you are commanded to **intentionally focus** on what is true, noble, and right. Name one specific Bible verse or spiritual truth you can memorize and immediately speak out loud the next time a debilitating worry about your family enters your mind.

- **Bearing Burdens (Galatians 6:2): Isolation** amplifies stress. Who is one person in your faith community — a pastor, elder, or trusted friend — with whom you can practice **bearing burdens** by sharing a genuine, unvarnished truth about your current struggles?

SECTION V: SUPPORTING FATHERS

CHAPTER 25
What Fathers Need

Many fathers find themselves facing **less than ideal circumstances.** Single, nonresidential, incarcerated, recovering, underemployed-the list goes on. Others are battling for parenting time. Perhaps one of those situations describes you or a father you care about.

Most are not "deadbeat." Many are simply beaten down by life because of poor decisions, generational poverty, addictions, and so on.

The responsibilities of shepherding their children remain, regardless of their circumstances. Unfulfilled by him, those responsibilities fall to the mother, other family, government, and society.

Many mothers do an amazing job with their children without much – if any - help from the fathers, but they shouldn't have to do it alone. That is not God's plan.

Many fathers who were poorly fathered become excellent parents because they vowed to give their children what they wish they'd had, a present, responsible, nurturing father.

In this final section, we will provide information about **the needs of fathers who want to be good family shepherds.** I will suggest ways the community can help them.

Five Greatest Needs

Recently, a colleague at a nearby Pregnancy Resource Clinic investigated the responses of 100 of their most recent client fathers regarding their greatest needs. With the assistance of AI, I analyzed their responses and found the following:

Based on the list, the five greatest needs of those fathers are:

1. **Financial Stability & Employment:** Many fathers expressed a need for a better-paying job, job security, and overall financial stability to support their family. This includes saving money and having the means to provide for a growing family's needs like housing, food, and baby supplies.

2. **Housing:** A significant number of fathers listed housing as a critical need, mentioning the desire for a stable home, a bigger house, or simply a place they can call their own. This reflects a fundamental need for a safe and secure environment for their family.

3. **Parenting Knowledge & Skills:** Many fathers want to learn how to be the "best dad they can be." This includes seeking advice on fatherhood, parenting skills, and understanding their role in a child's life.

4. **Partner & Child's Health:** Fathers are deeply concerned about the well-being of their partner and baby. Their needs include ensuring the mother and baby are healthy, getting regular doctor check-ups, and knowing how to support their partner during and after pregnancy.

5. **Personal Well-being:** This category includes a desire for self-improvement and mental health support. Fathers mentioned needing to be a better version of themselves, improving their physical health, managing stress, and dealing with personal issues like sobriety and mental health.

Analysis of Needs

The responses from the 100 fathers reveal a clear hierarchy of concerns, with tangible, immediate needs at the top. The most frequently mentioned needs fall into five core categories. These needs are not isolated but are interconnected. For example, a better job (financial stability) directly impacts the ability to secure better housing. Similarly, personal well-being, such as managing stress and self-improvement, impacts a father's ability to be a supportive partner and a good role model.

The breakdown of the needs is as follows:

- **Financial Stability & Employment (38 mentions):** This was the most prevalent theme. Fathers repeatedly mentioned needing a job, a better-paying job, or overall financial security. Examples include: "Finances," "Job," "Better paying job," and "To make sure I'm financially stable." This demonstrates that providing for their family is the primary concern for most fathers.

- **Housing (21 mentions):** Housing was the second most common need. Fathers expressed a clear desire for a stable, permanent home for their family. This includes mentions of "Housing," "House of our own," "Bigger House," and "Getting a place."

- **Parenting Knowledge & Skills (17 mentions):** This category highlights a strong desire to be an involved and effective parent. Fathers asked for "Parenting Advice," "Fatherhood Counseling," and a desire to "Learn how to be the best father I can be."

- **Partner & Child's Health (11 mentions):** A significant number of fathers were focused on the health and safety of their loved ones. Mentions included "Healthy Baby," "Making sure my Child's mom is healthy," and "Knowing for sure if she is pregnant and the steps afterward."

- **Personal Well-being (8 mentions):** This category, while less frequent, is still important. It reflects the internal struggles and goals of the fathers themselves, such as "Stay Sober," "Mental Health," "Become more motivated to work out," and "Working Hard."

The remaining needs, such as "Transportation," "Legal Status," and "Relationship Issues," were mentioned less frequently and were often tied to the larger five categories. For instance, a lack of transportation can be a barrier to securing a job and housing. Distilling this list into the top five "Greatest Needs" provides a clear picture of the primary challenges and concerns facing new fathers.

My next question was, how do these responses compare to national trends. Here is what I discovered:

The distilled needs from the survey of 100 local fathers closely align with the findings of national surveys and research on modern fatherhood. The core themes are remarkably consistent, showing that the challenges faced by this group of fathers are not unique but are part of a broader national trend.

Comparison to National Surveys

1. **Financial Stability & Employment:** This was the top need in the local survey, and it is consistently highlighted as a significant concern for fathers in national studies. Research from organizations such as the Pew Research Center and the National Fatherhood Initiative shows that being a "breadwinner" remains a primary role many men feel pressured to fulfill. Studies from 2024 and 2025 specifically point to the "cost of living crisis" as a significant source of financial pressure, which in turn impacts their mental health and family relationships.

2. **Housing:** While not always listed as a standalone category in national surveys, the need for housing is an integral part of the broader themes of financial stability and providing for the family. The desire for a bigger or more stable home is a direct consequence of a father's role as a provider, and it's a concern that underlies many of the financial anxieties mentioned in national reports.

3. **Parenting Knowledge & Skills:** My analysis of the local PRC survey's finding that fathers want to "learn how to be the best father I can be" is strongly supported by national data. Research indicates that **modern fathers are increasingly involved** in hands-on care and desire information on parenting skills, child development, and supporting their partner. This reflects a shift away from the traditional role of just being a provider to being a nurturing and emotionally present parent.

4. **Partner & Child's Health:** This need is also a significant point of comparison. National reports, such as a 2025 study on "Expectant and new fathers," show that fathers are deeply concerned with their baby's development and their partner's physical and mental well-being. This concern is so prevalent that some public health initiatives are now developing tools like the "Pregnancy Risk Assessment System for Dads" (PRAMS for Dads) to better monitor and support fathers' health during this transition.

5. **Personal Well-being:** Our finding on fathers' needs for mental and physical health is a critical and growing area of focus in national research. Surveys from 2024 and 2025 reveal that a significant number of dads are struggling with their mental health, often due to work-life balance issues and financial stress. The prevalence of paternal postpartum depression and anxiety is gaining recognition, with a key challenge being the stigma that prevents many men from seeking help. The need for personal improvement and self-care is a direct response to these stressors.

In summary, the needs of the 100 local fathers surveyed are not outliers. They reflect the major anxieties and aspirations of fathers across the United States. The desire to provide, the need for a stable home, the yearning for effective parenting skills, and the quiet struggle with personal well-being are all consistent and widely documented challenges for modern fatherhood.

Meeting The Needs of Fathers

It is essential to point out that the stated hierarchy of needs of these fathers is unselfishly focused on the needs of their families, and not on their personal well-being only. They accept responsibility for their child and the mother and are seeking help to fulfill those duties. It is only right that everything possible is done to support them.

The survey findings affirm the importance of the work of professional Fatherhood Practitioners and their agencies as they strive to identify the needs of the fathers they serve. But they cannot do it alone. It must be "all hands-on deck." The well-being of children is at stake.

Nearly 60% of the fathers surveyed have financial stability/employment concerns, as well as housing needs. Almost 20% have family and personal health needs. To address those anxieties, partnerships, collaborations, and referral relationships with government agencies, private social service entities, healthcare services, and other programs in the community are required. Unless it is part of a very large community agency that has most of those services in-house, partnerships are crucial to enabling fatherhood specialists to adequately serve fathers and families by connecting them to resources in their communities.

It is as those basic needs are being addressed that father-focused parent education and skill development programs can be most effective. The mobilization of multiple community sectors is recommended to adequately address the needs of fathers and families.

Representatives from housing, finance/banking, social/human services, healthcare, education, philanthropy, judicial, legal, and other sectors are needed at the table of collaboration to meet the needs of fathers of school-aged children and their parenting partners. Inspiration from the Holy Scriptures

But if anyone does not provide for his own, and especially for those of his household, he has denied the faith and is worse than an unbeliever. – 1 Timothy 5:8 NKJV

It is expected of a father to provide for his family. God has put the instinct within us to want to make sure that our children and wives are safe and have their needs met. Beyond our immediate families, Christians are also required to provide for relatives who are vulnerable or unable to provide for themselves, such as elderly or widowed family members. Failure to do so demonstrates a denial of Christian love and care, making one "worse than an unbeliever" because it contradicts the core principles of faith and love that even non-believers often practice.

The community helps itself when struggling fathers are supported as they endeavor to fulfill their God-given role as POPS (protector, order keeper, provider, and stabilizer).

Questions for Reflection and Discussion

Analyzing the Five Greatest Needs

- **The Hierarchy of Needs:** The survey showed that the top two needs were **Financial Stability (38%)** and **Housing (21%)**. Why are these two tangible needs, which directly address the father's role as a **Provider** (POPS), necessarily prioritized *before* categories like Parenting Skills or Personal Well-being?

- **The "Unselfish" Focus:** The chapter highlights that the hierarchy of needs is unselfishly focused on the needs of their families. If a father is actively struggling with **Personal Well-being** (e.g., sobriety, mental health), how can community support systems help him understand that addressing his *own* need is actually the **most responsible and loving action** he can take for his family?

- **Parenting Knowledge:** The desire to **"learn how to be the best dad they can be"** (17%) is a major need. If you were leading a fatherhood program, what is the single most valuable piece of knowledge or skill you believe a new father needs to immediately learn to be an **emotionally present and nurturing** parent?

- **Partner & Child's Health:** Fathers are deeply concerned about the well-being of their partner and baby. How can healthcare providers and hospitals better involve fathers in the prenatal and postpartum process to recognize and address their concerns, perhaps using tools like the **PRAMS for Dads** mentioned in the chapter?

The Call for Community and Spiritual Provision

- **The Shepherd's Responsibility (1 Timothy 5:8):** The Scripture states that a failure to provide for one's household is a denial of faith. How does the community's support of a struggling father allow him to *live out* this core biblical mandate, restoring his **dignity, purpose, and identity**?

- **The Interconnectedness of Needs:** The chapter notes that many needs are interconnected (e.g., transportation affects job security). If you had limited resources, which one need would you address first to create the **greatest positive domino effect** for a father seeking to fulfill his role as POPS (Protector, Order Keeper, Provider, Stabilizer)?

- **"All Hands-On Deck":** The text calls for the **mobilization of multiple community sectors** (housing, banking, healthcare, judiciary) to meet fathers' needs. If you were convening a table of collaboration in your community, which **two non-profit or government entities** would you prioritize inviting to address the dual needs of Financial Stability and Housing?

- **The Power of Example:** The chapter notes that many poorly fathered men become excellent parents because they vowed to give their children what they wish they'd had. If you were poorly fathered (or know someone who was), how did the **vow to be present and responsible** become a stronger motivation than generational poverty or poor decisions?

CHAPTER 26
What Noncustodial Fathers Need

In Chapter 25 we addressed some of the financial and employment, housing, parenting knowledge and skills, partner and child's health, and personal well-being needs of family shepherds.

In this chapter, we shift the focus to consider the circumstances and the needs of fathers who, for whatever reason, do not live in the same home as their children.

The special needs and challenges faced by noncustodial fathers are complex and multifaceted, encompassing emotional, legal, financial, and logistical aspects.

Special Needs and Emotional Challenges

1. **Emotional Distress and Grief:** Noncustodial fathers often experience significant feelings of **loss, grief, guilt, and separation anxiety** over not being a daily, physical presence in their child's life.

2. **Maintaining a Meaningful Bond:** There is a deep need to **preserve and nurture a strong, meaningful parent-child relationship** despite limited and often structured time. This requires consistency in communication during visits.

3. **Parental Authority and Influence:** Fathers need to maintain a sense of **parental authority and influence** in

their child's life, including being involved in major decisions (education, health, religion), which can be difficult without physical custody. Joint legal custody, where applicable, helps meet this need.

4. **Coping with Conflict:** They require strategies and support to **manage stress and anxiety** related to co-parenting conflicts, especially when disagreements or hostility with the custodial parent interfere with their time with the child.

5. **Addressing Stigma and Bias:** Some fathers feel they face a **societal or judicial bias** against them, leading to a need for emotional validation and assistance to counter the perception that a noncustodial father is inherently less important or capable than the custodial parent.

Challenges Getting Parenting Time (Visitation)

Noncustodial fathers often face specific hurdles that complicate or prevent them from exercising their court-ordered parenting time:

- **Parental Interference/Alienation:** The most significant challenge is often **direct or indirect interference** from the custodial parent, which can include:

    o   Denying or canceling visits without legitimate reason.

    o   Failing to make the child available for exchanges.

    o   Limiting or blocking communication (calls, video chats) between father and child.

- Withholding important information (school, medical records).

- Scheduling the child's activities (parties, sports) that conflict with the father's scheduled time.

- Parental alienation, which involves a parent attempting to turn the child against the other parent.

- **Logistical and Financial Hurdles:**

  - **Geographical Distance:** Relocation by either parent can make frequent visits impractical due to travel time and cost.

  - **Child Support and Finances:** The challenge of balancing child support obligations with personal finances while also covering the travel and activity costs associated with visitation. In some cases, access to the child can be correlated with being current on support payments, though courts generally view the issues as separate.

- **Legal Enforcement:** Many fathers need help with the complex and expensive process of **enforcing court-ordered parenting time** when the other parent is noncompliant, often requiring motions for contempt of court.

Support and Resource Needs

To address these challenges, noncustodial fathers require access to various resources:

- **Legal Assistance:** Affordable or free **legal consultation, information, and advocacy** to understand their rights, navigate family court, enforce parenting time orders, and seek modifications to custody agreements as circumstances change.

- **Co-Parenting Counseling/Mediation:** Services focused on **improving communication and conflict resolution** with the custodial parent, often through mediation or co-parenting counseling, to create a child-centered co-parenting plan.

- **Emotional and Mental Health Support: Therapy, counseling, and support groups** to help them process feelings of loss, guilt, and frustration, and develop healthy coping mechanisms for stress and anxiety.

- **Parenting Education:** Guidance on **maintaining a strong relationship from a distance** and effectively parenting during limited time, focusing on quality interactions and stability.

- **Help with Paternity Establishment:** For unmarried fathers, assistance with the process of **legally establishing paternity** to secure their rights to parenting time and decision-making.

If you have some or all of these services in your community, you are very fortunate. I encourage you to take full advantage of those resources. If your community is lacking programs and services for non-custodial parents, I recommend having conversations with your local county elected officials about this issue. You might consider beginning by rallying fellow taxpaying residents to add their voices to yours.

The following can be a starting point for discussions.

What Can Be Done to Assist Noncustodial Fathers

The best practices for helping noncustodial fathers are rooted in the principle that a child benefits from having a safe, meaningful, and consistent relationship with both parents. These practices, often championed by fatherhood programs, family courts, and social services, focus on four key areas:

1. Emotional and Mental Health Needs

- **Grief, Loss, and Emotional Stress**

    - **Best Practice:** Provide **Father-Specific Counseling and Support Groups**. Offer accessible mental health services, individual therapy, and peer support groups structured to validate the unique emotional challenges of noncustodial fatherhood (e.g., loss of daily interaction, feelings of being marginalized).

- **Lack of Parental Self-Confidence**

    - **Best Practice:** Use **Strength-Based Fatherhood Programs**. Utilize evidence-based curricula that help fathers identify their strengths, learn child development, and build confidence in their parenting abilities.

- **Maintaining Parental Identity**

  - ○ **Best Practice: Promote a "Parenting Partner" Mindset.** Encourage the father to reject the "Disneyland Dad" role and instead maintain consistent rules and routines during their parenting time, which reinforces their identity as a full parent, not just a visitor.

2. Maintaining the Father-Child Bond

- **Limited Face-to-Face Time**

  - ○ **Best Practice: Maximize Quality, Not Just Quantity.** Teach fathers strategies to make the most of their limited time by engaging in shared interests, creating meaningful traditions, and being fully present and attentive (e.g., no distractions).

- **Overcoming Distance**

  - ○ **Best Practice: Leverage Technology for Consistent Contact.** Establish clear guidelines in the parenting plan for consistent, non-interfered-with communication (video calls, phone calls, texts). Encourage the use of shared online activities (games, reading) to close the physical gap.

- Involvement in a Child's Life

    o **Best Practice: Facilitate Information Sharing and Participation**. Ensure the parenting order grants the noncustodial father direct access to the child's medical and school records. Encourage them to attend school events, parent-teacher conferences, and extracurricular activities whenever logistically possible.

3. Addressing Co-Parenting Conflict and Hostility

- High Conflict with Ex-Partner

    o **Best Practice: Mandate and Subsidize Mediation/Co-Parenting Classes**. Require both parents to attend structured co-parenting classes or professional mediation, focusing on child-centered communication skills and conflict resolution before returning to court.

- Interference/Gatekeeping

    o **Best Practice:** Encourage Use of **Neutral Communication Tools**. Promote the use of co-parenting apps (e.g., TalkingParents, OurFamilyWizard) that provide a verifiable, written record of all communication and scheduling, making it easier to hold a non-compliant parent accountable in court.

- Modeling Poor Behavior

  - Best Practice: "Business Partner" Communication. Instruct fathers to treat communication with the mother as a neutral, professional exchange focused only on the child's logistics, health, and education. Messages should be neutral in tone, informative, and to-the-point.

4. Legal and Logistical Hurdles

- Enforcing Parenting Time Orders

  - Best Practice: Provide Accessible Legal Resources. Establish Parenting Time Hotlines or legal clinics (often supported by state agencies) that offer free legal information and forms to noncustodial parents seeking to enforce or modify an order.

- Paternity Establishment

  - Best Practice: Integrate Paternity Services. Coordinate child support, social services, and legal systems to actively assist fathers in legally establishing paternity early, as this is the foundational step for securing all legal rights and court-ordered parenting time.

- Disputes Over Time

- o **Best Practice:** Utilize **Detailed Parenting Guidelines**. Courts should adopt and apply comprehensive, state-specific Parenting Time Guidelines that clearly define minimum time standards, holiday schedules, transportation responsibilities, and specific remedies (like "make-up time") for parental interference.

- **Legal Bias and Stigma**

  - o **Best Practice:** Promote **Gender-Neutral Language and Standards**. Courts should use terminology like "parenting time" (instead of "visitation") and apply the "best interests of the child" standard without a default preference for either parent, actively recognizing the value of two involved parents.

Instructions from the Holy Scriptures

[6] These commandments that I give you today are to be on your hearts. [7] Impress them on your children. Talk about them when you sit at home and when you walk along the road, when you lie down and when you get up. - Deuteronomy 6:6-7 NIV

Fathers are instructed by God to spend both quantity and quality interactions with their children, teaching and modeling for them constantly and consistently. When a father does not live in the same house as his child, that is unlikely to be the case. It is, nevertheless, important that fathers do everything they can to spend as much parenting time as possible with their child. The custodial parent is wise to encourage that and to be accommodating.

When that is not the case, communities and systems need to be in place to provide the support necessary to help noncustodial parents fulfill their God-given responsibilities for their children's well-being.

Questions for Reflection and Discussion

Emotional and Relational Needs

- **Emotional Distress and Grief:** The chapter states that noncustodial fathers often experience significant **grief, guilt, and separation anxiety**. If this describes you, what is the **most difficult emotional hurdle** to overcome when preparing for or concluding your parenting time? What specific steps do you take to process this loss in a healthy way?

- **"Disneyland Dad" vs. "Parenting Partner":** The best practice encourages noncustodial fathers to maintain a **"Parenting Partner" mindset** by keeping consistent rules and routines, rejecting the "Disneyland Dad" role. If your time with your child is limited, what is one **non-fun, routine-focused activity** (e.g., homework, chores, bedtime rules) you can commit to maintaining to reinforce your identity as a *full parent*?

- **Maintaining a Meaningful Bond:** Deuteronomy 6:6-7 instructs fathers to be constantly impressing wisdom on their children ("when you sit at home and when you walk along the road"). Since a noncustodial father's time is limited, how can he best leverage **technology (video calls, texts)** to fulfill this mandate and maintain that deep, consistent bond across the distance?

- **Lack of Parental Self-Confidence:** Noncustodial fathers may struggle with self-confidence due to limited time. How can **Strength-Based Fatherhood Programs** specifically help a father who feels marginalized identify and build upon his unique strengths as a parent?

Navigating Conflict and Legal Hurdles

- **Parental Interference: Parental interference/alienation** is cited as the most significant challenge. If you are a custodial parent, what is one way you can commit to being more **accommodating and encouraging** of the other parent's time, recognizing that the child benefits from a consistent relationship with both parents?

- **"Business Partner" Communication:** The best practice for managing high conflict is to treat communication as a **neutral, professional exchange** focused only on the child. Describe the characteristics of a text message or email about a child's medical appointment that would meet this **"Business Partner" standard**.

- **Co-Parenting Tools:** The chapter recommends using **Neutral Communication Tools** (like co-parenting apps). Why is having a **verifiable, written record** of communication and scheduling essential for protecting a noncustodial father's court-ordered rights?

- **Legal Stigma and Bias:** The chapter calls for the promotion of **gender-neutral language** (like "parenting time" instead of "visitation"). Why is this seemingly minor change in terminology important for affirming the **value and authority** of the noncustodial father?

Call to Action for the Community

- **Meeting Logistical Needs:** Noncustodial fathers face **Logistical and Financial Hurdles** (travel cost, support payments). If you are a community or church leader, what is one **legal or financial resource** you can establish or partner with (e.g., a free legal clinic, subsidized mediation) to address the need for **Accessible Legal Resources** and enforce parenting time?

- **Paternity Establishment:** Why is actively integrating services to assist unmarried fathers in legally **establishing paternity early** deemed the **foundational step** for securing *all* legal rights and court-ordered parenting time?

- **Accountability:** The community is called upon to provide the support necessary to help noncustodial parents fulfill their God-given responsibilities. What is the **first conversation** you, as an engaged resident or taxpayer, need to initiate with your local elected officials regarding the lack of services for noncustodial fathers in your area?

CHAPTER 27
Promising Practices for Churches (Part 1)

We prefaced *The Family Shepherd* by lamenting the fatherhood crisis in the Christian Church in America. In this chapter, we will zero in on what churches can do to strengthen fatherhood among their members.

Christian men who become godly servant leaders, in covenant with their spouses, work together to build strong families. Strong families help build solid congregations.

And that's only the beginning. Solid congregations contribute to healthy communities. Healthy communities are safer and more prosperous places for children and families. Safe and prosperous communities have better neighborhoods, effective schools, less crime, and on and on. That is living out Jesus' intent for His followers to be the salt and light of the world.

Salt and Light

13 "You are the salt of the earth; but if the salt loses its flavor, how shall it be seasoned? It is then good for nothing but to be thrown out and trampled underfoot by men.

14 "You are the light of the world. A city that is set on a hill cannot be hidden. 15 Nor do they light a lamp and put it under a basket, but on a lampstand, and it gives light to all who are in the house. 16 Let your light so shine before men, that they may see your good works and glorify your Father in heaven. – Matthew 5:13-16 NKJV

This is a powerful and foundational passage from Jesus' Sermon on the Mount, where He uses two vivid metaphors – salt and light – to describe the essential role and impact His followers have in the world.

In this passage, Jesus isn't just offering a nice sentiment; He's issuing a profound mandate. He tells His disciples – and by extension, all who follow Him – that they are intrinsically "the salt of the earth" and "the light of the world." This isn't a call to *become* something they are not, but rather to *live out* who they already are in Him.

"You are the salt of the earth": In ancient times, salt had several vital uses:

1. **Preservation:** It prevented decay and corruption. As salt, believers are called to be a preserving influence in a world prone to moral and spiritual decay. They are to stand against the forces of corruption and uphold righteousness.

2. **Flavor/Taste:** Salt enhances flavor. Christians are to bring a distinct, God-honoring "flavor" to society, making life richer and more meaningful through their character, values, and actions.

3. **Purification/Healing:** Salt had cleansing properties. Believers can bring healing and purification to broken systems and relationships.

The warning, "if the salt loses its saltiness," is stark. If followers of Jesus compromise their distinctiveness, if they blend in with the world to the point of losing their unique preserving and flavoring qualities, they become useless for the very purpose God intended for them. Their spiritual vitality is lost, and their impact becomes negligible.

"You are the light of the world": Light's purpose is to illuminate, guide, and dispel darkness.

1. **Revelation/Truth:** Light reveals what is true and exposes what is hidden. Believers are called to shine the truth of God's Word and the reality of His Kingdom into a world often shrouded in spiritual darkness, ignorance, and deception.

2. **Guidance:** Light helps people see where they are going. Christians are to be beacons of hope, offering moral and spiritual guidance to a lost and wandering humanity.

3. **Visibility:** A "town built on a hill cannot be hidden," nor should a lamp be covered. Our faith is not meant to be private or concealed. It's meant to be visible, lived out openly and courageously.

The command, "let your light shine before others, that they may see your good deeds and glorify your Father in heaven," emphasizes that our "light" is expressed through our actions. It's not about self-glorification or drawing attention to ourselves, but about living lives that are so distinctly righteous, loving, and good, that they point others beyond us to God Himself. Our transformed lives become a living testimony, leading others to acknowledge and praise the Source of all light.

Conclusion: Taken together, these metaphors are a powerful call to radical distinctiveness and proactive influence. Along with proclaiming the soul-saving gospel of Jesus Christ, living out our faith in our homes and communities as individuals and as families makes an eternal difference in the world. With support and encouragement, Godly fathers can and should play a key role in shepherding their families to fulfill the Lord's mandate to live as salt and light. In doing so, they contribute to preserving their communities from decay and dispelling the darkness by their presence.

Church-based fatherhood ministries play a vital role in strengthening families and communities by equipping men to be faithful family shepherds. In this chapter, I offer five promising practices for pastors and congregation leaders to create and sustain an effective fatherhood ministry.

I. Foundational Principles for Church-Based Fatherhood Ministry:

- **Biblical Focus:** Ground the ministry in biblical principles of fatherhood, emphasizing the father's role as family shepherd - spiritual leader, protector, provider, and guide for his family.

4 And you, fathers, do not provoke your children to wrath, but bring them up in the training and admonition of the Lord. – Eph. 6:4 NKJV

4 "Hear, O Israel: The Lord our God, the Lord is one! 5 You shall love the Lord your God with all your heart, with all your soul, and with all your strength.
6 "And these words which I command you today shall be in your heart. 7 You shall teach them diligently to your children, and shall talk of them when you sit in your house, when you walk by the way, when you lie down, and when you rise up. 8 You shall bind them as a sign on your hand, and they shall be as frontlets between your eyes. 9 You shall write

them on the doorposts of your house and on your gates. - Deuteronomy 6:4-9

- **Gospel-Centered:** Remind fathers of their identity in Christ, the Chief Shepherd, and the grace available to them. Acknowledge struggles and failures, offering hope and affirmation through the Gospel.

- **Disciple-Making:** View fatherhood ministry as a core part of discipling men to become intentional spiritual leaders in their homes and beyond.

- **Holistic Approach:** Address not only spiritual growth but also practical aspects of shepherding - parenting, marriage, finances, personal well-being, and more.

- **Community and Accountability:** Foster a safe space for men to share their joys and struggles, build deep friendships, and hold each other accountable.

II. Engaging Fathers:

- **Start Simple and Informal:** Don't over-structure initially. Begin with informal gatherings like breakfasts, barbecues, or "drop-in" socials to build relationships and trust.

- **Relational Engagement:** Prioritize personal invitation and genuine connection. Pastors and leaders should create opportunities for men to speak openly without fear of judgment.

- **Address Felt Needs:** Identify common challenges and concerns among fathers in your congregation (e.g., balancing work/family, discipline, spiritual leadership) and tailor content to those needs.

- **Normalize Struggle:** Use preaching and testimonies to show that spiritual struggle is everyday and growth is an ongoing process.

- **Public Affirmation:** Publicly affirm and commission fathers during worship services, reminding them of their sacred calling.

Getting Your Church Started

Suppose you are interested in starting or growing a father-focused ministry for discipling men in your church to be family shepherds. In that case, we recommend that you begin by praying, seeking wisdom and guidance from The Great Shepherd, the Creator of family, while looking to the Holy Scriptures for inspiration.

We can help you create a strategy for bringing your God-given vision into practical reality and implementing these best practices with your team. Reach out to me to start a conversation. Fatherhood ministry can revolutionize your church by helping to build strong families who impact your community for God's glory. Email me personally at ewilliams@urbanlight.org.

Instruction From The Holy Scriptures

The righteous man walks in his integrity;
His children are blessed after him. - Proverbs 20:7 NKJV

This verse emphasizes the importance of living a life of integrity, which is rewarded not only for the individual but also for their descendants. Living with integrity means being honest, fair, and upright in all one's dealings and decisions. The verse emphasizes the positive impact of a righteous life on future generations. The promise is that children who witness and are raised by a parent who lives with high character are more likely to inherit those same values and experience positive outcomes in their own lives.

Intentional father-focused ministry helps dads become, not perfect, but positive examples of principled family shepherding that can benefit not only his children, but his family for generations to come.

Questions for Reflection and Discussion

The Mandate of Salt and Light

- **Distinctiveness and Preservation:** Jesus commands followers to be **"the salt of the earth"** (Matthew 5:13), meaning they should prevent moral and spiritual decay. How does a father's **integrity and spiritual leadership** in his home directly serve as a "preserving influence" (salt) that prevents corruption in his family's values?

- **Visibility and Glorifying God:** Our faith is meant to be visible (a **"light of the world"**). What is one **"good deed"** or visible expression of faith and love in your family life that, if seen by your community, would cause them to **"glorify your Father in heaven"**?

- **Losing Saltiness:** The warning is stark: if the salt loses its flavor, it is useless. What is the greatest **"compromise"** or area where Christian fathers tend to blend in with the secular culture (e.g., priorities, work ethic, media consumption) that causes them to lose their **distinctive spiritual flavor**?

Foundational Principles for Ministry

- **Biblical Focus (Ephesians 6:4, Deuteronomy 6:4-9):** The ministry must focus on the father's role as the **spiritual leader and guide**. What is one **specific spiritual practice** (e.g., family devotion, blessing children, shared prayer) that you currently incorporate—or need to start incorporating—to fulfill the command to **"bring them up in the training and admonition of the Lord"**?

- **Holistic Approach:** A fatherhood ministry should address not only spiritual growth but also practical aspects (**parenting, marriage, finances**). If your church were to offer one new class based on a **felt need** (a practical problem men are facing), which topic would you suggest, and why?

- **Disciple-Making:** How is viewing fatherhood ministry as a core part of **discipling men** fundamentally different from simply offering a "**parenting class**"? How does this shift in perspective elevate the father's role?

- **Community and Accountability:** The ministry must foster a **safe space** for men to share joys and struggles. What key characteristic must the *leader* of this group demonstrate (e.g., vulnerability, non-judgment) to build the deep **trust and accountability** necessary for men to open up?

Engaging Fathers and Lasting Impact

- **Start Simple and Informal:** If you were launching a fatherhood ministry, what **simple, informal gathering** (e.g., breakfast, barbecue, service project) would you use to build initial **relational engagement and trust** before introducing formal teaching?

- **Normalize Struggle:** How can **pastoral preaching and public testimonies** be used to normalize struggle and acknowledge failure, thereby reducing the shame and stigma that prevents many fathers from seeking help or community?

- **Integrity and Legacy (Proverbs 20:7):** The righteous father's children **"are blessed after him"** due to his integrity. What is one **principled decision** you can make today, in your work, finances, or family time, that models high character and will **positively impact your children and future generations?**

CHAPTER 28
Promising Practices for Churches
(Part 2)

As I suggested in Chapter 27, impactful congregations are foundational to healthy communities. Healthy communities, in turn, provide safer and more prosperous environments for children and families. This positive cycle results in better neighborhoods, more effective schools, reduced crime, and so much more—a true reflection of Jesus' command for His followers to be "the salt and light of the world."

I recommended two best practices for effective church-based fatherhood ministry: setting the groundwork with foundational principles and developing a plan for engaging fathers.

In this chapter, we'll delve into three more promising practices for building and sustaining an effective church-based fatherhood ministry.

Promising Practices

III. Equipping Family Shepherds:

- **Provide Resources and Tools:** Offer practical, easy-to-use resources like family prayer cards, short devotionals, Bible reading plans, and Christian parenting guides.

- **Workshops and Classes:** Host workshops and seminars on specific topics, such as:

- Understanding a father's biblical role.

- Effective discipline methods.

- Nurturing a child's spiritual growth.

- Marriage enrichment.

- Balancing work and family.

- **Mentorship Programs:** Facilitate connections between older, experienced fathers and younger dads. This can be one-on-one or through facilitated small groups.

[17] *As iron sharpens iron,*
   so one person sharpens another. – Proverbs 27:17 NIV

This proverb highlights the idea that interactions with other men can improve and refine a person's character and parenting skills, just as one piece of iron can sharpen another.

- **Integrate into Existing Ministries:** Incorporate fatherhood-focused content into your men's ministry, small groups, and Sunday school classes.

- **Sermon Application:** Regularly feature applications for fathers in sermons, not just on Father's Day.

IV. Empowering Fathers:

- **Vision Casting:** Give fathers a clear vision for their role as shepherds in their homes and the impact they can have on their children and generations to come.

- **Leadership Opportunities:** Invite fathers into visible leadership roles within the church and family-focused ministries, allowing them to use their gifts and grow.

- **Accountability Circles:** Create small groups or "huddles" where dads can pray for each other, share challenges, and provide mutual encouragement.

- **Encourage Self-Care:** Remind fathers of the importance of their own spiritual, emotional, and physical well-being. (More on that in the next chapter.)

- **Long-Term Vision:** Emphasize that fatherhood ministry is a long-term commitment, fostering ongoing growth and support.

V. Practical Activities & Ideas:

- **Father-Child Activities:** Organize events that strengthen the bond between fathers and their children, such as:

  - Sporting events

  - Camping trips

  - Building/crafting projects

  - Community service projects

  - Family worship nights

- **Peer Support Groups:** Create dedicated groups for young fathers to share experiences, challenges, and successes.

- **Resource Library:** Establish a collection of books, materials, and online resources on parenting, marriage, spiritual development, and servant leadership.

- **Informal Discussion Topics:** Use simple, appealing discussion topics to spark conversation, such as

"Balancing work and family life" or "Overcoming common parenting challenges."

- **Anonymous Q&A:** Allow dads to submit questions anonymously for discussion among more experienced dads.

By implementing these promising practices, churches can create robust and impactful fatherhood ministries that equip men to shepherd their families with conviction, humility, and love, ultimately strengthening the church and beyond.

Resources

Several organizations and approaches emerge as highly effective in supporting church-based fatherhood ministries. These typically provide resources, training, and a framework for local churches to implement their own programs.

Here are four prominent examples that offer significant support for churches:

1. **Manhood Journey:** This organization is highly focused on equipping fathers to be disciple-makers in their homes. They offer a wealth of resources, including video-based courses, Bible studies for fathers and sons, and customizable fatherhood events. They emphasize a holistic approach to fatherhood, addressing spiritual, relational, and practical aspects. Many churches partner with Manhood Journey to utilize their curriculum and training for their men's and fatherhood ministries. https://manhoodjourney.org/

2. **Kingdom Dads:** Their goal is to transform culture by equipping dads to love and lead their families toward God's kingdom. In partnership with Christian churches, schools, and workplaces, Kingdom Dads equips small group cohorts of dads to walk through intentional and Gospel-centered practices together. Their partnership and small group cohort model are the heart of their ability to pursue faithfulness together. https://kingdomdads.org/

3. **Fathers in the Field:** With a unique focus on mentoring fatherless boys, this ministry equips churches to recruit and train "Mentor Fathers" who commit to a long-term relationship with a fatherless boy, providing spiritual guidance, practical skills, and a positive male role model. This program is powerful for churches looking to directly impact the fatherless within their communities and provides a structured model for mentorship. https://www.fathersinthefield.com/

4. **Fathering Strong, powered by Urban Light Ministries:** The ministry offers many resources for fathers, including bible-based courses, devotionals, books, a weekly podcast, a weekly blog, and more. ULM also offers the Fathering Strong® mobile app, which helps build virtual communities of fathers dedicated to supporting one another through their fathering and faith journeys, ultimately building stronger families and communities. As a powerful accompaniment to in-person groups, fathers can build online communities to share stories, share prayer requests, offer help to others and get the support they need 24/7/365.

ULM assists churches in developing comprehensive church-based fatherhood ministries that are customized for their congregations. https://urbanlight.org/

Key Characteristics of Successful Church-Based Fatherhood Ministries (drawing from these and other effective models):

- **Biblically Grounded:** They emphasize the spiritual calling of fathers.

- **Relational and Mentorship-Focused:** They prioritize building strong connections among men and creating opportunities for mentorship.

- **Practical and Equipping:** They offer tangible resources, skills, and training that help fathers in their everyday lives.

- **Supportive and Encouraging:** They create a non-judgmental environment where fathers can be open about their struggles and receive encouragement.

- **Integrated with the Church:** They are not a separate silo but are woven into the fabric of the church's overall ministry to men and families.

Many churches also develop their own unique programs, often drawing inspiration and resources from organizations like those listed above to fit their specific congregational needs.

Instructions From the Holy Scriptures

4 And you, fathers, do not provoke your children to wrath, but bring them up in the training and admonition of the Lord. Ephesians 6:4 NKJV

And now a word to you parents. Don't keep on scolding and nagging your children, making them angry and resentful. Rather, bring them up with the loving discipline the Lord himself approves, with suggestions and godly advice. – Ephesians 6:4 TLB

This verse emphasizes fathers' responsibility to raise their children in a way that avoids angering them and actively nurtures their spiritual life. Since many fathers were not raised this way, churches are advised to provide training in biblically based male nurturance.

Questions for Reflection and Discussion

Equipping and Empowering Family Shepherds

- **Iron Sharpening Iron (Proverbs 27:17):** The text emphasizes **Mentorship Programs**. If you were a new father, what is the **most valuable trait or piece of advice** you would seek from an older, experienced father? If you are an experienced father, what is the most important lesson you would share with a younger dad?

- **Training and Admonition (Ephesians 6:4):** The church is advised to provide training in **biblically based male nurturance** to help fathers avoid provoking their children to wrath. What specific **workshop or class topic** (e.g., "Effective Discipline Methods," "Nurturing Spiritual Growth") do you believe is most critically needed by fathers in your congregation today?

- **Vision Casting:** The ministry should give fathers a clear vision for their role as shepherds and the **long-term impact** on generations. How does the church effectively communicate that a father's **daily, quiet consistency** is just as vital as public spiritual leadership?

- **Leadership Opportunities: Empowering Fathers** involves inviting them into visible leadership roles. What is one **specific, visible role** within the church or a family ministry that could best utilize a father's practical gifts (e.g., teaching, organizing, building) and reinforce his shepherd identity?

Practical Application and Integration

- **Father-Child Activities:** The text suggests activities that strengthen the father-child bond. Beyond sporting events, what is one **meaningful, non-competitive activity** (e.g., a service project, a building/crafting project) that the church could organize to facilitate **quality, shared time** and create lasting memories?

- **Integration into Existing Ministries:** Fatherhood ministry should be woven into the **fabric of the church**. What is one simple way a men's ministry or a sermon series could consistently **Integrate Fatherhood-Focused Content** without making it a separate, isolated program?

- **Accountability Circles: Accountability Circles** or "huddles" provide mutual encouragement. What is the most crucial element needed to ensure these small groups remain a **safe, non-judgmental space** where men feel comfortable sharing challenges and prayer requests?

- **Anonymous Q&A:** Allowing dads to **submit questions anonymously** addresses the reluctance many men have to show vulnerability. What practical, low-tech system (e.g., a submission box, an online form) could your church use to facilitate this process effectively?

Successful Ministry Characteristics and Resources

- **Key Characteristics:** Successful ministries are **Relational, Practical, and Biblically Grounded**. Which of the four organizations listed (Manhood Journey, Kingdom Dads, Fathers in the Field, Fathering Strong) seems to best align with the **specific needs and ministry style** of your church, and why?

- **Mentoring the Fatherless (Fathers in the Field):** The Fathers in the Field model focuses on equipping men to **mentor fatherless boys**. Why is a structured, long-term commitment to a fatherless boy considered a "powerful" way for a church to directly impact its community and live out the "light of the world" mandate?

- **24/7 Support (Fathering Strong App):** The use of a mobile app to build virtual communities offers fathers **24/7/365 support**. How does this use of technology help overcome the **Isolation** that often amplifies stress for fathers who are unable to consistently attend in-person meetings?

CHAPTER 29
Self Care of the Family Shepherd

Working from Rest

"Everybody's working for the weekend," says the once-popular 80s song by the Canadian rock band Loverboy. Come Friday night, many people are exhausted from work. Then, on Saturday, yard work, car washing, and endless household chores begin. Come Sunday, there's often more to do, and then it's back to the grind the next morning. It seems we are working for a weekend that includes very little proper rest.

While the topic of rest was addressed earlier, this chapter builds on the concept of work/life balance by focusing on the critical need for **quality rest**. For us as fathers and shepherds of our homes, rest is not a luxury; it is a spiritual, emotional, and physical necessity.

Tired of Being Tired? The Reality of Burnout

Are you among the millions experiencing burnout? Studies suggest it is alarmingly common among American workers, highlighting a serious issue that impacts not just job performance, but also marriage and family life.

A few statistics illustrate the widespread nature of this problem:

- In a 2021 survey by the American Psychological Association, up to **79% of workers** reported experiencing work-related stress.

- A separate VoiceNation survey indicated that **70% of respondents** claimed to have experienced workplace burnout.

- In yet another survey, **79% of employees** reported experiencing work-related stress in the past month.

These figures highlight widespread burnout, which can significantly affect your life far beyond the workplace. When a father is burned out, the adverse ripple effect on the family unit can be profound.

Burnout's Impact on Your Marriage and Family

Burnout directly undermines your ability to be a present and effective shepherd in your home:

- **Reduced Emotional Availability:** Emotional exhaustion — the core symptom of burnout — leaves you with less emotional energy for your partner and children. You might become withdrawn, less patient, or struggle to connect meaningfully.

- **Increased Conflict:** Exhaustion and frustration easily turn into irritability and resentment. Simple disagreements can escalate due to a lack of patience and emotional bandwidth.

- **Neglect of Family Responsibilities:** Feeling constantly drained makes it difficult to fulfill household chores, childcare duties, or participate in quality family time. This creates feelings of burden and resentment among other family members.

- **Strained Communication:** Burnout can cause communication to suffer. You might become withdrawn or short-tempered, leading to misunderstandings and a communication breakdown.

- **Reduced Intimacy:** Burnout can significantly decrease a person's libido and interest in physical intimacy, further straining the marital relationship.

- **Impact on Children:** Witnessing a parent experiencing burnout can be stressful for children. They might feel neglected, confused by changes in your behavior, or even take on some of the emotional burden of the suffering parent.

Overall, burnout creates a negative ripple effect within the family unit, leading to feelings of isolation, disconnection, and dissatisfaction for all members.

Recovering from Burnout and Prioritizing Self-Care

Unfortunately, there isn't a one-size-fits-all cure for burnout. Recovery involves addressing the root causes and rebuilding your resilience. As the shepherd, you must prioritize your own well-being to effectively care for your flock.

Here are key strategies to consider for your recovery:

- **Address the Source:** Reflect on what's causing your burnout. Is it work overload, lack of control, a bad work environment, or personal struggles? Identify the stressors so you can start tackling them.

- **Set Boundaries:** Learn to say "no" and delegate tasks when possible. Establish clear boundaries between work and personal life to avoid constant work encroachment.

- **Seek Support:** Do not bottle up your feelings. Talk to a trusted friend, family member, therapist, or counselor. Having a support system is crucial for recovery.

- **Lifestyle Changes:** Make changes to reduce stress, such as spending more time in nature, engaging in hobbies you enjoy, or pursuing social activities that bring you joy.

- **Reevaluate Your Work:** Sometimes, the best solution is to make changes at work. Talk to your manager about your workload, explore opportunities for flexible work arrangements, or consider a career shift if necessary.

- **Professional Help:** If you're struggling to manage burnout on your own, do not hesitate to seek professional help from a therapist or counselor who specializes in stress management and burnout recovery.

The Power of Rest

Focus on activities that nurture your mind, body, and soul. This must include **prioritizing getting enough rest**. Rest is essential for our well-being because it allows our bodies and minds to recharge and repair themselves. Just like a machine needs downtime for maintenance, so do we.

- **Physical Health:** During rest, our bodies rebuild tissues, strengthen muscles, and repair injuries. Adequate sleep is crucial for this process. It also helps regulate hormones that affect metabolism and weight management.

- **Mental Well-being:** Rest allows our brains to process information, consolidate memories, and improve focus. When well-rested, you experience better emotional regulation, reduced stress, and a more positive mood, making you a calmer father and husband.

- **Immune System:** Rest strengthens our immune system, making us less susceptible to illness. Chronic lack of sleep can weaken the body's defenses.

Overall, prioritizing rest is an investment in your health and happiness. It allows you to function physically, mentally, and emotionally at your best.

Work from Rest, Not Exhaustion

There's a world of difference between working from a place of rest and working from exhaustion. Approaching your work and family responsibilities from a rested state is far more valuable and Christ-honoring:

- **Enhanced Focus and Productivity:** When well-rested, your brain can concentrate better, absorb information more easily, and think critically. This translates to fewer errors and better decision-making at work, and more mindful presence at home.

- **Improved Creativity:** Rest allows your mind to wander and make unexpected connections. This is where innovative solutions and insightful counsel for your family often spark.

- **Greater Resilience:** Feeling rested makes you better equipped to handle challenges and setbacks. You will have more emotional stamina to deal with stress and maintain a positive attitude with your spouse and children.

- **Stronger Motivation:** Approaching life from a rested state allows you to find the energy and motivation to tackle your day enthusiastically, both professionally and personally.

- **Reduced Risk of Burnout:** Constantly pushing through exhaustion is a recipe for burnout. Working from rest allows you to maintain a sustainable pace and avoid feeling overwhelmed.

Daily and Weekly Rest

Daily rest is critical. Experts recommend that most adults aim for between **7 and 9 hours of sleep each night**. This range acknowledges that individual needs can vary slightly.

To prioritize rest also means setting aside one day a week—for most of us, Sunday—as a day of rest. Commit to doing no unnecessary work to allow your body and mind to recover from the previous week's toll and be strengthened for the week ahead.

Plan to attend worship service to restore your soul and spirit. Rested and rejuvenated on Sunday, you will have the spiritual and physical strength to carry you through the week.

Make Rest a Family Commitment

As the shepherd of your home, discuss with your household the importance of quality rest for *every* family member. The sooner your children commit to adequate rest, the healthier they will grow to be as adults. Set a healthy example by prioritizing your own rest and showing them that stopping to recharge is a sign of wisdom, not weakness.

Remember: Prioritizing rest is an investment in your and your family's health and happiness. It allows us to function physically, mentally, emotionally, and spiritually at our best. Approaching life and work from a rested state empowers us with the energy and motivation to tackle each day enthusiastically.

Inspiration from the Holy Scriptures

Ultimately, the deepest rest we can experience is in the provision and grace of God. Jesus offers a rest that goes beyond the physical and permeates the soul:

"Come to me, all you who are weary and burdened, and I will give you rest. Take my yoke upon you and learn from me, for I am gentle and humble in heart, and you will find rest for your souls. For my yoke is easy and my burden is light." — Matthew 11:28-30

Here are some practical, expert-backed tips for better sleep hygiene:

Establish a Consistent Routine

- **Stick to a Schedule:** Go to bed and wake up at the same time every day, including weekends. Consistency reinforces your body's natural sleep-wake cycle (circadian rhythm), making it easier to fall asleep and wake up feeling refreshed.

- **Set a Wind-Down Hour:** Start relaxing at least an hour before your target bedtime. This signals to your brain that it's time to slow down. Follow the same calming steps each night (e.g., wash face, read, stretch).

Create a Sleep-Friendly Environment

- **Make Your Bedroom a Haven:** Reserve your bed primarily for **sleep and intimacy**. Avoid working, watching TV, or using your laptop in bed, so your brain strongly associates the space with rest.

- **Dark, Cool, and Quiet:** Keep your room as **dark, quiet, and cool** as possible. A temperature around 65 to 68 degrees is often ideal. Consider using blackout curtains, earplugs, or a white noise machine if necessary.

- **Ditch the Screens:** Avoid prolonged use of light-emitting screens (phones, tablets, computers, TV) for **at least an hour** before bed. The blue light suppresses the production of melatonin, the hormone that promotes sleep.

Mind What You Consume

- **Watch Caffeine and Nicotine:** Avoid caffeine and nicotine for at least **4 to 6 hours** before going to bed, as they are stimulants that interfere with sleep.

- **Limit Alcohol:** While alcohol may initially make you feel sleepy, it disrupts your sleep quality later in the night. Avoid it for several hours before bedtime.

- **Eat Wisely:** Avoid going to bed hungry or stuffed. Refrain from heavy, large, or spicy meals within a couple of hours of bedtime. If you need a snack, opt for something light.

Manage Your Day and Your Worries

- **Exercise Regularly:** Regular physical activity promotes better sleep, but try to avoid intense exercise within an hour or two of your bedtime, as it can be stimulating.

- **Limit Naps:** Long daytime naps can interfere with nighttime sleep. If you must nap, keep it to less than an hour and avoid napping late in the day.

- **Manage Stress:** If worries keep you up, try to resolve them before bedtime. Jot down what's on your mind or create a to-do list for the next day, and then "set it aside" until morning. Relaxation techniques like meditation or deep breathing can also help ease anxiety.

When You Can't Sleep

- **Get Up and Try Again:** If you don't fall asleep within about 20 minutes of going to bed, **get out of bed** and do something calming and non-stimulating in dim light, like reading a book. Only return to bed when you feel sleepy again. Avoid clock-watching, as this creates anxiety.

A Final Word on Self-Care

To conclude this chapter, remember that **self-care is not selfish—it is foundational.**

The core principle of prioritizing rest and working from a state of well-being can be summed up with a familiar piece of advice, often heard from airline flight attendants:

"Put on your oxygen mask first, before you try to help your child."

In a crisis, a father's first responsibility is to ensure he can **sustain his own capacity to act**. If the cabin pressure drops, and you try to secure your child's mask while you pass out from lack of oxygen, you fail both of you.

Your Capacity is Your Family's Security: As the shepherd of your family, your physical, emotional, and spiritual health represents the stability of your household. If you allow yourself to be constantly worn down by exhaustion and stress, you are essentially reducing your own oxygen supply.

- **A Burned-Out Father Cannot Shepherd:** You won't be much of a family shepherd if you wear yourself down, get sick, or become emotionally unavailable. You need a full battery to lead with patience, wisdom, and energy. **Caring for yourself is caring for your family.**

The Example of the Good Shepherd

Even Jesus, the Good Shepherd, understood the necessity of rest and withdrawal. The Gospels frequently record Jesus stepping away from the crowds and His demanding ministry to find quiet time for rest, prayer, and renewal with the Father. He even took naps. Be like Jesus!

If the Son of God prioritized rest to sustain His work, how much more must you, a busy, fallible father, do the same? **Working from rest** is simply following the model of the greatest servant leader who ever wore a human body. It is an act of stewardship over the life and body God has entrusted to you, ensuring you remain strong, present, and capable for those who depend on you most.

Questions for Reflection and Discussion

The Reality of Burnout and Its Impact

- **Burnout Self-Assessment:** The core symptom of burnout is **emotional exhaustion**. Which of the three major impacts — **Reduced Emotional Availability, Increased Conflict, or Neglect of Family Responsibilities** — is the most pronounced symptom of exhaustion in your home life right now?

- **Working for the Weekend:** The chapter contrasts working from exhaustion with **"Working from Rest."** On a typical Monday morning, do you feel more like you are working from a state of **rest and enthusiasm** or from a state of **drain and obligation**? What is one specific activity you do on Saturday that prevents you from entering your week rested?

- **The "Oxygen Mask" Principle:** The chapter uses the analogy, **"Put on your oxygen mask first."** If your capacity is your family's security, what is the **greatest risk** your family faces when you consistently neglect your own need for sleep and self-care?

- **Impact on Children:** How have your children reacted to witnessing you experiencing burnout (e.g., confusion, withdrawal, taking on emotional burden)? What is one thing you can do this week to show them that **stopping to recharge is a sign of wisdom, not weakness**?

Strategies for Rest and Recovery

Addressing the Source: Recovery starts with addressing the root cause. Do you believe your burnout is primarily due to **work**

overload, **lack of control** over your circumstances, or **personal struggles** (e.g., anxiety, physical health)? What is the *first boundary* you need to set (at work or at home) to tackle this source?

- **The Sabbath Principle:** The chapter recommends committing to a day of rest (or one full day/period weekly). If you commit to doing **no unnecessary work** during this time, what is one non-essential activity (chore, work email) you will **intentionally postpone** to prioritize spiritual and physical recovery?

- **Sleep Hygiene (Ditching the Screens): Blue light** from screens suppresses the sleep hormone melatonin. If you commit to avoiding light-emitting screens for an hour before bed, what **calming, non-stimulating activity** (e.g., reading a physical book, stretching, writing) will you adopt as your new wind-down routine?

- **Setting Boundaries:** What is one responsibility or chore that you could realistically **delegate to your spouse or children** this week to free up some of your limited emotional bandwidth?

The Spiritual Model of Rest

- **Rest for the Soul (Matthew 11:28-30):** Jesus offers rest that permeates the soul: **"Come to me, all you who are weary and burdened, and I will give you rest."** How does turning your **weariness and burdens** over to Christ differ from merely "taking a nap," and how does that spiritual rest affect your **patience** as a father?

- **The Example of Jesus:** Even the Son of God prioritized rest and withdrawal. When you look at Jesus' model, what is the **most challenging temptation** you face that keeps you from following His example of stepping away for **quiet time for rest, prayer, and renewal**?

- **Stewardship of the Body:** Prioritizing rest is an **act of stewardship** over the life and body God has entrusted to you. What is one **lifestyle change** (exercise, nutrition, managing stress) you will implement as an act of good stewardship to ensure you remain strong and capable for your family?

CHAPTER 30
Conclusion

In writing *The Family Shepherd*, I set out to explore the work of shepherding – from Middle Eastern sheep herders to the Divine Shepherd, and congregational shepherds of the Body of Christ. In doing so, I sought to draw a parallel to the calling of fathers to be faithful, loving, humble, and courageous shepherds of their families.

I hope you were inspired by the shepherd's commitment, sacrifice, and servant leadership, and found inspiration, insight, and practical instruction here for godly fathering. I desire that on these pages, you found information and discovered resources that will help you on your family shepherding journey.

If you are a pastor or other leader of a Christian congregation, I hope Section V stimulated and equipped you with ideas for beginning or strengthening a fatherhood ministry within your church.

Turning the Hearts of Fathers

With the tragic fatherhood crisis in the Church and the world, there is a desperate need for a movement that turns fathers' hearts toward their children and families. May the promised reconciliation of fathers and children be fulfilled in our lifetime.

Behold, I will send you Elijah the prophet
Before the coming of the great and dreadful day of the Lord.
6 And he will turn

The hearts of the fathers to the children,
And the hearts of the children to their fathers,
Lest I come and strike the earth with a curse." – Malachi 4:5-6

The Family Shepherd: *Guiding, Serving, and Protecting Your Flock with Love, Courage, and Enduring Faith* seeks to encourage fathers to take an active role in leading their families, as the Divine Shepherd models for us. I pray you were so inspired.

References

[i] https://manhoodjourney.org/wp-content/uploads/2025/05/State-of-Biblical-Fatherhood-Report.pdf
[ii] https://urbanlight.org/fathering-strong/
[iii] www.todaysnewhope.org
[iv] Chifamba, E. (2014). A Strategy to Train Local Church Elders for Effective Assimilation and Nurture of New Converts. https://doi.org/10.32597/dmin/262/
[v] Chifamba, E. (2014). A Strategy to Train Local Church Elders for Effective Assimilation and Nurture of New Converts. https://doi.org/10.32597/dmin/262/
[vi] Ephesians 4:11-16
[vii] https://www.skyquestt.com/report/adult-entertainment-market
[viii] https://www.unicef.org/harmful-content-online#:~:text=Pornographic%20content%20can%20harm%20children.,violence%2C%20and%20other%20negative%20outcomes.
[ix] https://www.cdc.gov/child-abuse-neglect/about/index.html#:~:text=Quick%20facts%20and%20stats,3
[x] https://urbanlight.org/fathering-strong/
[xi] https://www.selfinjury.bctr.cornell.edu/
[xii] https://autism.org/self-injury/#:~:text=ARI's%20free%20self%2Dinjurious%20behavior,online%20app%20to%20learn%20more.

[xiii] Discover the Power of Fathers as Servant Leaders - Urban Light Ministries. https://urbanlight.org/discover-the-power-of-fathers-as-servant-leaders/

[xiv] Group Cohesion | The Nexus Initiative. https://www.thenexusinitiative.com/connectionnexus/group-cohesion

[xv] For a comprehensive look at the meaning of love (agape), read my book **Father Love – The Powerful Resource Every Child Needs** 2nd edition. https://fatherlovebook.com/ Available on Amazon https://a.co/d/bdO6VFz

[xvi] https://www.hhs.gov/surgeongeneral/reports-and-publications/parents/index.html#:~:text=Reports%20and%20Publications-,Parental%20Mental%20Health%20%26%20Well%2DBeing,and%20Well%2DBeing%20of%20Parents

[xvii] https://psychiatryonline.org/doi/10.1176/appi.pn.2025.02.2.12#:~:text=A%20recent%20Surgeon%20General's%20advisory,Getty%20Images%2FiStock%2Furbazon

To learn more about Church-based Fatherhood Ministries or the additional resources that accompany this book please go to:

www.urbanlight.org